Out in Paperback is a wonderfully entertaining look at gay mass-market paperback cover art that throws new light on the important role of the book publishing industry in the development of gay popular culture. Richly illustrated with over a hundred covers of gay-themed "pulps" published between 1948 and 1998, this fascinating visual history provides new insights into a striking form of gay imagery.

Following the huge demand for portable reading material during World War II, paperback publishing exploded in the postwar years. At the same time, the Kinsey report and a spate of novels and non-fiction studies about male homosexuality suggested new and sensational subject matter. Literature, mass culture, and the emerging homosexual underground combined in the accessible pulp paperback with its striking, interpretive packaging. For many readers – including young, isolated gay men–an eye-catching, pocket-sized paperback cover on a drugstore rack provided their first intriguing look into a previously concealed gay world.

What were the messages behind the emblematic images and flashy graphics? For whom were they intended? What was their impact on a rapidly changing North American society? Ian Young, author of *The Stonewall Experiment: A Gay Psychohistory* and an authority on gay publishing, probes beneath the surface of gay pulp covers to reveal their underlying, sometimes surprising, messages.

MLR Press Authors

Featuring a roll call of some of the best writers of gay erotica and mysteries today!

Derek Adams	Z. Allora	Maura Anderson
Simone Anderson	Victor J. Banis	Laura Baumbach
Helen Beattie	Ally Blue	J.P. Bowie
Barry Brennessel	Nowell Briscoe	Jade Buchanan
James Buchanan	TA Chase	Charlie Cochrane
Karenna Colcroft	William Cooper	Michael G. Cornelius
Jamie Craig	Ethan Day	Diana DeRicci
Vivien Dean	Taylor V. Donovan	Theo Fenraven
S.J. Frost	Kimberly Gardner	Michael Gouda
Kaje Harper	Alex Ironrod	Jan Irving
David Juhren	AC Katt	Thomas Kearnes
Sasha Keegan	Kiernan Kelly	K-lee Klein
Geoffrey Knight	Christopher Koehler	Matthew Lang
J.L. Langley	Vincent Lardo	Anna Lee
Elizabeth Lister	Clare London	William Maltese
Z.A. Maxfield	Timothy McGivney	Tere Michaels
AKM Miles	Reiko Morgan	Jet Mykles
William Neale	Cherie Noel	Willa Okati
Brynn Paulin	Erica Pike	Neil S. Plakcy
Rick R. Reed	A.M. Riley	AJ Rose
George Seaton	Riley Shane	Jardonn Smith
DH Starr	Richard Stevenson	Liz Strange
Marshall Thornton	Lex Valentine	Haley Walsh
Mia Watts	Missy Welsh	Stevie Woods
Ian Young	Lance Zarimba	Mark Zubro

Check out titles, both available and forthcoming, at
www.mlrpress.com

Out In Paperback

A Visual History of Gay Pulps

Ian Young

mlrpress
www.mlrpress.com

Published by
MLR Press, LLC
3052 Gaines Waterport Rd.
Albion, NY 14411

Visit ManLoveRomance Press, LLC on the Internet:
www.mlrpress.com

Cover Art by Paul Richmond
Interior Layout by Kris Jacen
Editing by Judith David

Print format ISBN #978-1-60820-560-8
Ebook format ISBN#978-1-60820-561-5

Re-issued 2012

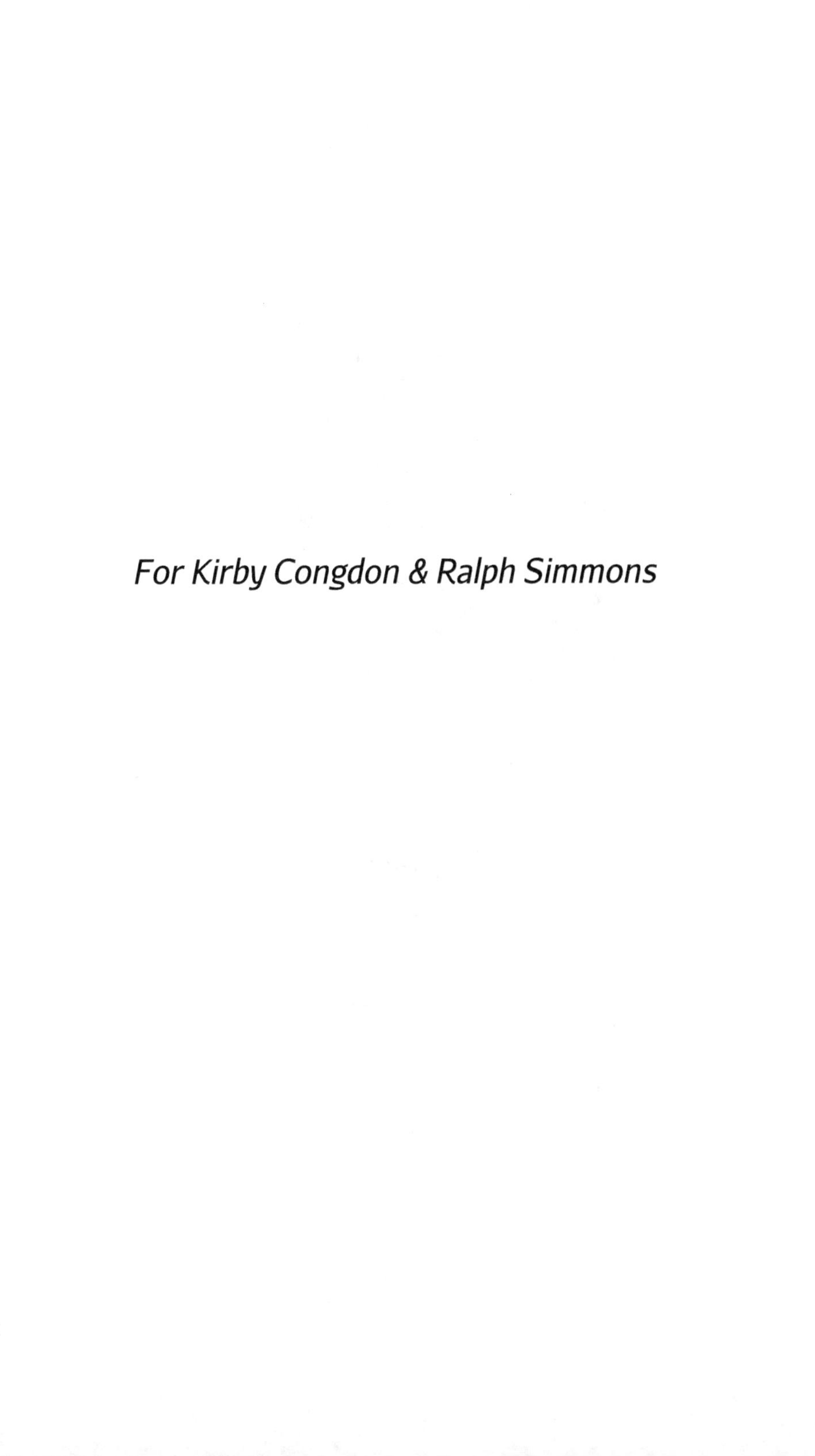

For Kirby Congdon & Ralph Simmons

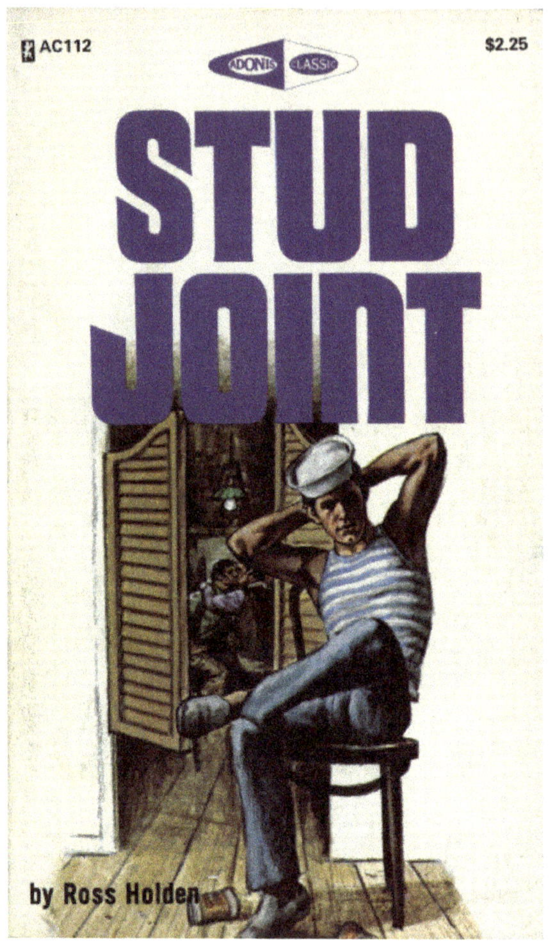

Ross Holden.
Stud Joint (Greenleaf Classics, 1975)

A Note to the Reader

You are now entering "...a world of forbidden passion, a hidden world of twilight men with secret signals and strange passions - half-men incapable of love as most men know it, yet harboring a burning need that drives them to forbidden acts performed on moonlit beaches, handsome men caught in the violent, shadowy world of the third sex, a pastel world of furtive pleasures, fey relationships, unconventional sex and hidden shame, a half-world of men who are different! Half in secret, half in the open, they walk the divided path, prowling the byways of hidden desire for a love that defies society's strongest taboo. It can happen to anyone! One day a man with a family - the next day, plunged into the twilight world of homosexuality, torn between the demands of the flesh and the dictates of the heart, wrestling with demons and forbidden desires, enslaved to the overpowering masculinity of a lean, hard-muscled, hot-blooded male with the face of an angel and the body of a wild stallion. Searing! Shocking! Blazing! Intimate! Uncompromising! A love that dare not speak its name."

Quotation assembled from cover blurbs on gay paperback novels.

I would like to thank Wulf, John S. Gray, Robert Wilson, David Mason, Carl Stryg, Paul Richmond and the late Richard George-Murray for their various contributions. Earlier versions of parts of this book appeared in *The Gay & Lesbian Review Worldwide, Torso, Stallion* and *The Golden Age of Gay Fiction*. All the books depicted are from the author's collection.

All books depicted are from the author's collection.

Contents

Introduction: *How Gay Paperbacks Changed America*

In an era when gay books are widely published and available, it can easily be forgotten that not so many years ago - well within the span of a lifetime - the subject of homosexuality was a media taboo. The breakthrough came after World War II, when gay writing suddenly emerged from the shadows to enlighten and scandalize a naive public. The new Homophile movement of the Fifties and Sixties was accompanied by an unprecedented upsurge of gay literature, and particularly of gay novels, in both Britain and America. At a time when gay magazines reached only a small number of people and gay themes seldom made their way into radio or film, gay novels provided just about the only public information on homosexuality apart from sensationalist newspaper accounts of prosecutions and scandals.

The pioneering authors of post-war gay fiction met with considerable resistance. Gore Vidal's postwar gay novel *The City and the Pillar* was denied advertising space; James Baldwin's agent refused *Giovanni's Room;* gay books and magazines were put on trial for obscenity. These were relatively minor matters compared to the grim fate of writers in the East Bloc. But in both Cold War camps, new voices strained to be heard.

The vicissitudes of advertising policy, the timidity of literary agents and even the attitudes of the courts were of interest to only a small segment of the American public. Most people in small (or even large) towns knew nothing of these matters, and seldom saw any of the notorious books in question. That is, not until they came out in paperback and showed up on a rack in the local drugstore, soda shop or dime store. For many isolated young gays, that eye-catching 7" x 4¼" cover of *Whisper* or *Rough Trade* provided the first window onto the gay world.

The rise of homophile movements in the US and Britain occurred at precisely the same time as the Anglo-American paperback explosion. The wide availability of cheap paperback books helped spread the word about sexuality and a way of life that, until the war years, had been largely hidden from public view. Postwar paperbacks played an important role in the social and political developments of the Cold War years, strongly reflecting and influencing the emerging gay consciousness. Cheap, easily available paperbacks were as important to changing attitudes in the pre-Stonewall era as gay magazines and poetry chapbooks were in the Gay Liberation years that followed.

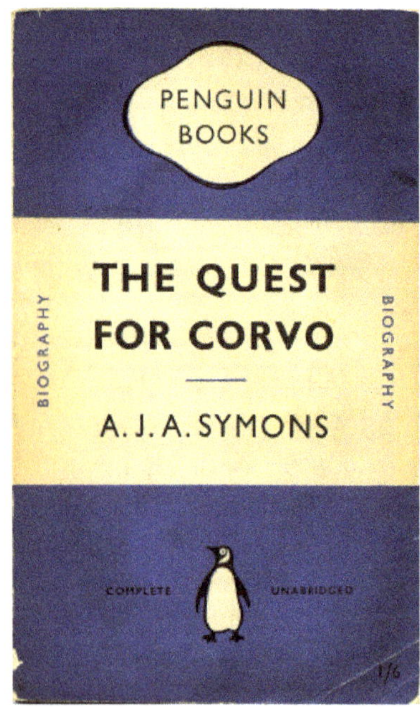

A.J.A. Symons
The Quest for Corvo (Penguin, 1940)
Early Penguins set the pattern for the mass-market paperback format. Their distinctive designs could be seen from across a railway platform.

In the West, *de facto* censorship could be surmounted by innovative technology to deliver the goods in a new way - and consequently, to produce a new kind of goods. In the totalitarian society of the East Bloc, tight legal censorship had to be countered by a lonely, fearful trek backward to make innovative use of the technology of the past. The difference was in the distribution. In the West, where the means of distribution remained in private hands, new entrepreneurial approaches had a chance to develop. In the Soviet Union and the East Bloc, with distribution controlled by a central government, forbidden texts were secretly retyped and furtively circulated in carbon copies as *Samizdat* - "self-publishers" - an ironic play on the State Publishers *Gosizdat.* America and the West prospered. The East Bloc stultified.

Throughout the Cold War years, a steady stream of gay books scandalized, titillated and enlightened readers in North America and Britain: from the Southern gothics of Carson McCullers and Truman Capote in the late Forties, through a long roster of novels and the eye-opening *The Homosexual in America* in the Fifties to Christopher Isherwood's restrained *A Single Man* and the raunchy hustling stories of John Rechy and "Phil Andros" in the Sixties.

Some of these titles were initially published in hardcover, but relatively few people had a chance to hear of them, and many bookstores - and even libraries - did not stock them. An early example of this new species of American literature, Charles Jackson's *The Fall of Valor*, a sombre study published in 1946, was one of many that failed to make it through the gauntlet of censorious librarians. "Subject, and especially bluntness of presentation," warned the *Library Journal*, "limit library use." Three years later, *Kirkus Reviews* sniffed that as Nial Kent's treatment of the gay theme in *The Divided Path* was "overt" rather than "fastidious," it was therefore a novel only "for the sensation seeker" who presumably should not be encouraged to ascend the steps of the library.

Busy pharmacists, Woolworths proprietors, malt shop managers and owners of general stores were seldom burdened by these high-minded considerations. If a rack of garish paperbacks showing guys with guns, busty babes and an occasional pair of half-naked men could boost profits, there were few objections. Paperbacks - both original titles and reprints from hardcover editions - were an innovation that allowed new gay literature to proliferate and find its readers outside the traditional bookshops and lending libraries. Out in paperback, gay literature found a younger, more diverse readership.

Though the widely distributed, mass-market paperback was a 20th century innovation, relatively inexpensive paperbound books had circulated in Europe as early as the 17th century. The invention of the steam rotary press and the proliferation of railroad lines in the 19th century allowed books to be produced and distributed cheaply and in large numbers. "Penny dreadfuls" and "dime novels" became enormously popular. And more dignified literary productions like the simple, elegant Tauchnitz and Albatross lines were promoted to the new breed of continental and intercontinental traveler, the jet-setters of their day. The invention of the typewriter produced an even greater outpouring of popular fiction. The Library of Congress has nearly 40,000 different 19th century dime novels, from 280 different series and countless authors, many using several pen-names. Horatio Alger published his influential boys' morality adventures in this format - paperbound on cheap stock that tends to discolor, turn brittle and crumble with time.

By the 1890's, dime novels were beginning to be superceded by the many so-called "pulp magazines" like *The Black Mask.* The heyday of the pulps, and pulp authors like Cornell Woolrich, lasted into the 1940's when World War II brought mass market paperbacks into their own again. In 1929, the American publisher Charles Boni pioneered a modest paperback line using a subdued, tasteful format and striking cover illustrations by Rockwell Kent. Haldeman-Julius' cheaply produced Little Blue Books and the orange-jacketed titles of Britain's Left Book Club each filled a specific need. But the real 20th century breakthrough into mass sales was made by the Englishman Allen Lane with his Penguin Books in 1935. The Depression had caused sales of Lane's publishing firm The Bodley Head to plummet, and the first ten titles of the now famous paperback line were introduced to turn things around.

The experiment was a great success. The original Penguins employed superior type, paper and ink and plain but distinctive covers. Savings came through large print runs and sales at newspaper kiosks and railway stations all over Britain. Penguin soon opened a US office, and the foundation for the post-war paperback boom was laid.

The war itself, which changed so much for America and Britain gave paperbacks an enormous boost. To satisfy the Allied troops' hunger for portable reading material, the official Armed Services Editions were devised, with titles ranging from Melville, Whitman and Housman to useful tracts like *Danger in the Cards: How to Spot a Crooked Gambler.* A total of 1,322 titles were distributed free to the troops, many in print runs of over 10,000 copies. From this experiment, many men who had never before read for pleasure developed a taste for literature of one sort or another. The ex-servicemen who helped form the first Homophile organizations - and the first leather clubs - were among those readers. As were women, nudged out of their traditional roles by the war.

In post-war America, publishers like Popular Library, Fawcett Gold Medal and Ace (which published William S. Burroughs' first book, the quasi-autobiographical *Junkie*, bound back-to-back with a vice cop's memoirs) were all competing for what had quickly developed into a hot new market. In Britain, Pan, Corgi and Foursquare became important postwar paperback houses.

In the Forties, Fifties and Sixties, America's traditional sexual mores struggled to free themselves from pre-war standards. The Kinsey reports - one on men released in 1948, the other on women released in 1953 - shattered the silence that allowed so many misconceptions about homosexuality to persist. The old attitudes about the Love that Dare Not Speak Its Name were finished. But, newly publicized, homosexuals now became suspect beings, targets of Cold War paranoia.

Whispers of homosexuality surrounded the crucial

Hiss-Chambers espionage case in 1948. Three years later, the revelation that two defecting British diplomats were homosexuals added fuel to the fire. In 1950, Wisconsin senator Joe McCarthy began a series of mendacious attacks on homosexuals and supposed communists in government. The chairman of the Republican National Committee echoed the widely held view of the day that "perhaps as dangerous as the actual Communists are the sexual perverts who have infiltrated our government." Hearst reporters Jack Lait and Lee Mortimer took up the cry in their popular book *Washington Confidential*, denouncing "dull, dumb deviates...twisted twerps in trousers" lurking in the "mediocrity and virtual anonymity" of the civil service. They claimed that "young students" were being systematically "indoctrinated" in Soviet Russia and "given a course in homosexuality." Seizing the political advantage, McCarthy stepped up his anti-homo witch-hunt, aided by attorney Roy Cohn and FBI Director J. Edgar Hoover. All three, as it happened, were themselves deep closet cases. Britain too saw an alarming rise in anti-gay frame-ups and prosecutions, culminating in the imprisonment of Lord Montagu and journalist Peter Wildeblood in 1954.

British gay campaigner Allan Horsfall recalled the atmosphere of the time: "One felt that the police were ubiquitous and omniscient with their spy-holes and the secret surveillance and their *agents provocateurs* and their trawls through people's private diaries and letters...Had it been conceivable to produce a gay man's survival guide at that time," he added, "it would have urged him never to reveal his name or address, never to discuss how he earned his living or where he worked, never to take anybody to his home or give anybody his telephone number and never to write letters, whether affectionate or not, to anybody with whom he was sexually invovled or even to anybody he knew to be gay. Many gay men, of course, did some or all of these things and remained untouched by the law. But their untroubled survival was due to good luck rather than wise behaviour."

Dr R.W. Reid described the police "going round from house to house [in English towns], bringing ruin in their train, always attacking the younger men first, extracting information with lengthy questioning and specious promises of lighter sentences as they proceed from clue to clue, i.e. from home to home." Many gay men fled abroad (if they could afford it) or destroyed incriminating personal papers.

Parallel to these events was the steady, year-by-year appearance of a series of revelatory gay novels. In 1951, Pyramid Paperbacks issued a revised version of Nial Kent's *The Divided Path,* and two years later *The Heart in Exile* by "Rodney Garland" appeared at the height of the scandals. Many gay titles peppered the paperback racks in the years following, as the new Homophile movement grew in the US and homosexual law reform started to be discussed in Britain. The 1950's also saw a profusion of lesbian pulp novels (now documented by Jaye Zimet's *Strange Sisters*), and in the Sixties, erotic gay paperback fiction became more widely available.

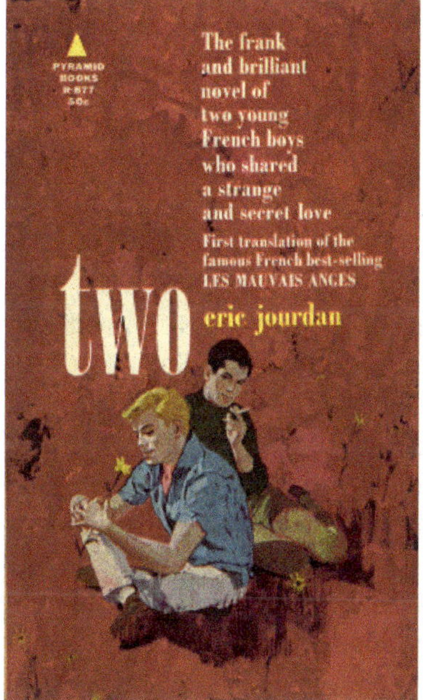

Eric Jourdan
Two (Pyramid, 1963)
The first gay pulp I ever bought - a steamy French novel about two cousins who ride their motorbike off a cliff. I was 18 when it hit the dime store racks in a come-pick-me-up cover by Mort Engel.

These new "mass market" paperbacks were not promoted by reviews, literary critics, librarians or educators. Produced in standard pocket-sized formats and displayed on stout, rotating wire racks or face out on store shelves, their colourful covers served as their advertisements. Many pulpy reprints of Zola's *Nana* and collections of O. Henry stories were sold by garish cover illustrations of well-endowed females bursting out of their bodices. Then as now, living authors had no more control than dead ones over cover art. Sometimes, gay novels were given hetero covers; James Colton's *Lost on Twilight Road* (National Library, 1964) showed a half-naked woman ripping the clothes off a stunned-looking man. Only the code word "twilight" in the title suggests what it's really about. But most publishers soon abandoned this approach. Paperback covers became more explicit, sometimes better designed and more attractive than their hardcover equivalents.

From the late 1940's into the 21st century, paperback books disseminated millions of images of homosexuals all over America - images that were at once both public and private. A paperback book designed to be carried in the pocket (one of the leading publishers was *Pocket Books*), is first seen publicly on the drugstore rack, and later read in private or even in secret, often at night (many fantasy dreamboys had their origins in paperback cover art). Americans were introduced to the realities of homosexual life not by radio or TV, nor by *The New York Times* or the Mattachine Society, but by the paperback revolution that brought gay and lesbian books into every American town. In 1966 there was even a book called *The Homosexual Explosion.* At a time when public images of gay men were rare, pocket-sized paperbacks gave homosexuality enormous visibility. Widely available and sold for as little as 35c each, paperbacks were within reach of the public - both financially and literally.

Facilitating this gay paperback explosion was a series of important American legal judgements. A 1953 ruling permitting distribution of European writer Tereska Torres's novel *Women's Barracks,* which included a number of notorious lesbian passages, suggested that lesbian literature was not necessarily illegal. A flood of lesbian pulp novels followed, all of them with provocative covers appealing to readers of both sexes. In 1957, Lawrence Ferlinghetti's publishing house City Lights was put on trial for distributing its paperback edition of Allen Ginsberg's poem "Howl," vigorously defended by the American Civil Liberties Union. Further trials involved the homophile magazine *One* and several pictorial gay magazines published by Guild Press of Washington, DC, which published beefcake magazines as well as more literary productions.

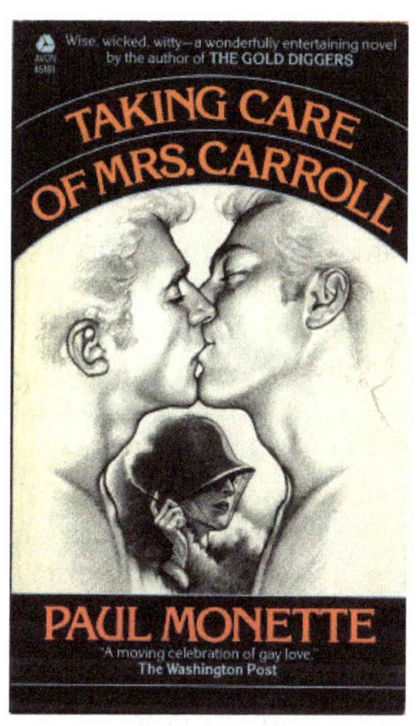

Paul Monette
Taking Care of Mrs. Carroll (Avon, 1979)
Pulp covers rarely showed men kissing. One that did was this novel from the late Seventies.

By the time the US Supreme Court had ruled in favor of freedom of the press, commercialism was already seizing its opportunity, and gay books proliferated from both literary and "porno" publishers. One of the earliest and best writers in the field was Samuel Steward whose "Phil Andros" hustling stories were published by Greenleaf Classics and Frenchy's Gay Line. Piracy was sometimes a problem for legally dubious material. Steward's *San Francisco Hustler* was ripped off by Cameo Library who reprinted it as *Gay in San Francisco* by "Biff Thomas" - though the inclusion in the pirate edition of a chapter excised from the original edition raised unanswered questions. While Steward/Andros dealt with male prostitution, rough trade and S/M, another writer of Sixties erotica, Carl Corley, specialized in romantic stories of boys from the country. He adopted a distinctive camp/kitsch style to illustrate his own covers, which bore titles like *Cast a*

Wistful Eye.

The well-known French publisher Maurice Girodias issued a number of English-language gay books that made their way to America. Girodias took great care with the appearance of his books, whose covers were often elegantly conservative in appearance. An edition of *The Young & Evil,* the classic novel of New York gay life in the Thirties by Parker Tyler and Charles Henri Ford, featured a wrap-around cover with a delicious black-&-white photo of a reclining near-naked young man. Later Girodias' US imprint issued the non-fiction gay guide *The Homosexual Handbook,* around the time of the Stonewall rebellion. Threats of retribution by J. Edgar Hoover and conservative columnist William F. Buckley, Jr. led to their names being removed from the second edition's "grapevine line-up" of famous homosexuals.

The leading publisher of gay erotica in the Sixties and Seventies was Phenix/Greenleaf Classics whose later productions adopted a distinctive H-format cover style. It was Greenleaf who in 1970 issued the first post-Stonewall anthology of contemporary gay literature, E.V. Griffith's *In Homage to Priapus.* Greenleaf was also responsible for Richard Amory's 1966 bestseller *Song of the Loon,* a "gay pastoral" about love and sex between white men and Indians in the American wilderness. This Leatherstocking tale with the sex put back in became the most famous of all gay erotic novels, at least prior to the arrival of John Preston's *Mr. Benson* fourteen years later. *Song of the Loon*'s wrap-around cover design avoided both the old "people of the shadows" stereotype and the blatantly sexual approach that would become standard for later gay porn. It showed a bearded white man in buckskins kneeling by a young, flute-playing Indian against a backdrop of mountains, reeds and white willows. The book was such a hit it inspired a paperback parody called *Fruit of the Loon*.

The popularity of *Song of the Loon* and its several sequels pointed to a mass market eager for gay romance, and semi-retired novelist Gordon Merrick stepped into the breach. *The*

Lord Won't Mind and its various follow-ups featured soap-opera plots and gay heroes gifted with spectacular endowments both anatomical and financial. Most of these were published as paperback originals by Avon, one of the largest New York paperback houses. The romantic-realist covers created for the series by artist Victor Gadino broke with convention by featuring men reaching out to each other or showing overt affection. They too were displayed in supermarket bookracks all over America.

With a respectable house like Avon venturing into soft-core gay erotica, a number of companies came along to rival Greenleaf's hard-core efforts. Surree House's "HIS 69" series featured drawings of near-naked boy-next-door types, usually in pairs. Rough Trade's leather and S/M titles were distinguished by the publisher's trademark black and orange covers which often incorporated the drawings of the well-known illustrator "Rex". Another of the Seventies erotica publishers was Blueboy Library; associated with the popular magazine of the same name, Blueboy Library published a number of titles by "John Ironstone" combining gay erotica with political themes.

But by the early Eighties, the tide had begun to turn for gay paperback porn. Legal and economic changes led to the demise of the leading Seventies publishers. AIDS altered sexual attitudes and mainstream commercial presses were publishing more gay-oriented novels. When Larry Kramer's *Faggots* appeared in paperback, you could choose from several cover colours, perhaps to coordinate with your living room decor. In the 1990's Masquerade Books' Badboy and Hard Candy editions took over where Greenleaf and the other porn publishers had left off, and began publishing reprints and more literary books as well.

More gay books are now published in the larger Trade Paperback format (approximately 8 ½" x 5 ½") though some still appear as Mass Market paperbacks. Some of the gay paperbacks of the past have survived and are still to be found cheaply in junk shops and secondhand bookstores. They are starting to be recognized as important cultural artefacts, their changing images of gay men faithfully documenting the evolution of popular views and beliefs. A first edition of Carl Corley's *The Purple Ring* now fetches over $100, and the price for a first edition *Song of the Loon* is climbing even higher. Savoured when they appeared, often taken for granted or discarded later, gay paperbacks are beginning to acquire a nostalgic, Antiques Roadshow glamour, while retaining all their pulpy "reach out and buy me" appeal.

A Visual History of Gay Pulps
1948 - 1998

What follows is a brief illustrated chronicle, decade by decade, of half a century of popular paperback books about homosexual and bisexual men.

The first "pulps" - magazines of short, popular fiction published before the Second World War - were often published in Digest format - approximately 7¼" tall by 5¼" wide.

Though this format was occasionally used by some early paperback publishers, the 7" x 4¼" format pioneered by Allen Lane's Penguin Books proved more enduring. The mass market paperbacks published in Britain and North America generally appeared in this format, or a slightly smaller "pocket size" of 6" x 4¼".

Appropriately, the earliest book listed in the brief history of mass-market gay paperbacks that follows is a commentary on the first Kinsey Report of 1948, *Sexual Behavior in the Human Male*. In the decades to come, many non-fiction books about male homosexuality, from the scholarly to the sensationalistic, were issued or reissued in mass market paperback. Anti-gay polemics like Pat Boone's *Coming Out*, published by Bible Voice, Inc. with a screaming woman on the cover, vied with pro-gay polemics like Rev. Troy Perry's *The Lord is My Savior and He Knows I'm Gay*. Memoirs, histories and biographical studies included accounts of the trials of Oscar Wilde and Roger Casement, and photo-illustrated quickie celebrity biographies.

Most of the books discussed are fiction - novels or short stories - and fall into one or another of several categories. Authentic gay pulp fiction, usually published as paperback originals, consists of soft-core novels - sensational without being pornographic - with such titles as *Summer in Sodom, Rough Trade* and *Strange Marriage.* A number of authors specialized in this genre, among them Carl Corley, K.B. Raul, Joseph Hansen (in his pseudonymous early career) and the briefly prolific Jay Greene. Literary fiction (usually reprints of hardcover editions) includes titles by well-known writers like Christopher Isherwood, Angus Wilson, James M. Cain and Frank Yerby. Genre fiction includes mysteries, science fiction, fantasy, westerns, stories for young adults and a few other categories of lesser significance. Then there is straightforward pornography, exemplified by titles like *Cock Cult* and *Biker in Bondage.*

Of course, each category contains works of varying quality. Some authors transcend their packaging; publication by a porno company was one way to avoid literary censorship. "Phil Andros," " John Ironstone," William Talsman, Marco Vassi, Philip José Farmer and Samuel R. Delany all published erotic books with further dimensions that distinguished and expanded the genre.

The field is littered with pseudonyms. "David Griffin," author of the creepy obsession novel *The Wrong People* (Paperback Library, 1967) outed himself in 1973 as Robin Maugham in a new Pan edition with a Preface by Cyril Connolly. "Phil Andros" was both character and author; the author half was Samuel M. Steward, variously an English professor and a tattoo artist known as Philip Sparrow. "Billy Farout" was the poet William Barber. "James Colton" was Joseph Hansen. Gore Vidal published his gay novel over his *own* name - and used a pseudonym for *Death in the Fifth Position*, a ballet mystery with a padded crotch and just a whiff of lavender. And "J. Watson," author of the revelatory *The Sexual Life of Sherlock Holmes*, was also, as Larry Townsend, author of *The Leatherman's Handbook.*

Many pseudonymous authors remain unidentified to this day.

But this is a study of cover art, and so is primarily a visual history. To paperback firms, even more than to hardcover publishers, book covers were enormously important. To a large extent, it was the cover art that sold the book, or at least interested the browser enough to pick it up and turn it over: back cover blurbs were also important. From the earliest days, many pulp paperback illustrators were accomplished artists. James Avati, James E. Bama, Jennifer Eachus, Gilbert Fullington, Raymond Johnson, Robert Jonas, Mel Odom and Barye Phillips were leading names in the field. And a porno book with a cover by Rex, Toby or Tom of Finland was sure to outsell its rivals. Works by many of these artists - and by many artists who remain obscure or anonymous - are illustrated here.

Even people who never bought a gay paperback nevertheless encountered the covers with their all-important pictures, face out on drug-store and dime-store racks. Those pictures and their underlying patterns and recurring motifs, illustrate not only the books they adorn but also some of Western culture's broadly shared ideas and beliefs about what for centuries had been "the abominable crime not to be mentioned among Christians," upon which no man might safely gaze.

The Forties

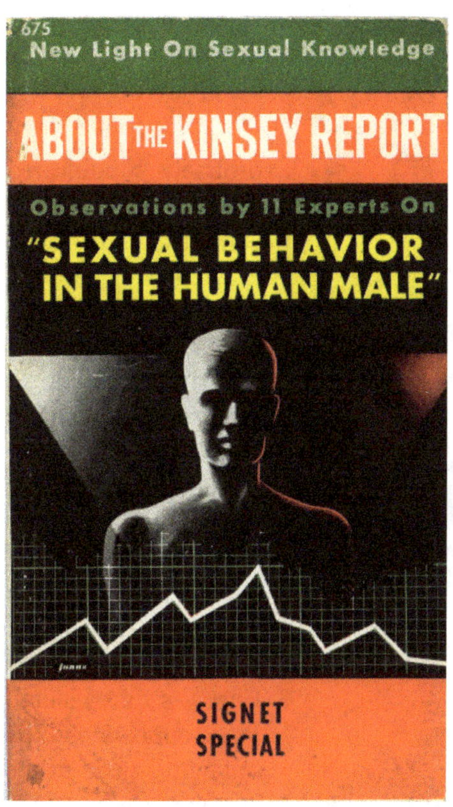

Donald Porter Geddes and Enid Curie (eds.) *About the Kinsey Report* (Signet Special, 1948).

In 1948, a small medical press published a massive volume of sexual research by an eccentric former gall-wasp scholar, Dr. Alfred Kinsey. Years in the making, this breakthrough volume, *Sexual Behavior in the Human Male,* showed that the practice of male homosexuality was not restricted to a few men on the margins of society but was rather widespread among white American manhood. Before Kinsey, homosexuality was seldom discussed in the American press, and then usually inaccurately, but "The Kinsey Report" received extensive press all over America and Kinsey's public lectures attracted thousands. Though the Kinsey study itself never appeared in paperback, several commentaries on it did, including *About the Kinsey Report*, which was rushed to press before the end of the year. People who would never have thought of buying a dubious-looking novel might buy a sober-seeming study of the much-discussed Report. Published commentaries on Kinsey, even when hostile, broke the homophobic taboo and

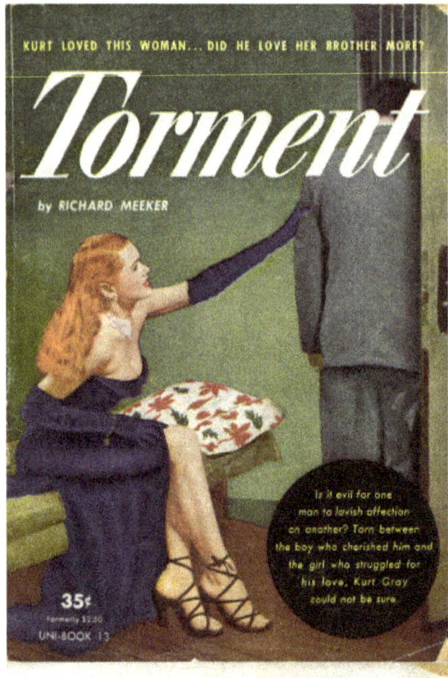

Richard Meeker - *Torment* (Uni-Book, undated) (front & back)

spread previously inaccessible information and inconceivable ideas.

Undated but probably published in the late 1940's or early 1950's in the 7 ½" x 5 1/4" "digest" format popular before the War, *Torment* was a retitled reprint of Richard Meeker's 1933 novel *The Better Angel* featuring motifs that would recur on later mass-market novels with gay content: the Disconsolate Man and the Consoling Woman. Here, a grey-suited man appears to be hiding his head in the curtains as a leggy lady in high-heeled lace-ups reaches out to him. The blurb ("Torn between the boy who cherished him and the girl who struggled for his love...") is fairly straightforward. The back cover promises both "Forbidden Ecstasy" and "a mass of impropriety," perhaps in an attempt to cater to all points of view.

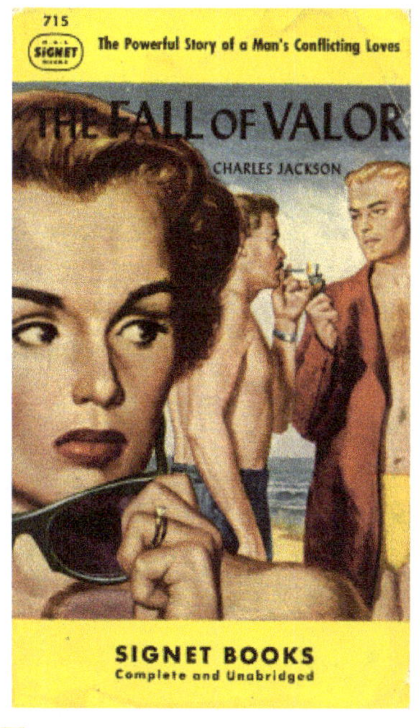

Charles Jackson
The Fall of Valor (Signet, 1949)

The Fall of Valor, by the author of *The Lost Weekend,* was one of the breakthrough American gay novels of the immediate post-war period. Signet's cover shows a motif - rare for the time - of two men face to face. A woman, fidgeting with engagement and wedding rings, looks on apprehensively. Many early covers depicted this triangle of two men and a woman. Homosexuality and bisexuality were frequently seen as disturbing and threatening to heterosexuality and marriage.

Carson McCullers
Reflections in a Golden Eye (Bantam, 1950)

Carson McCullers's *Reflections in a Golden Eye* was one of the first novels with significant gay incident to be accepted by a major mainstream publisher, Houghton Mifflin. Bantam's 1950 reprint employed a striking, quasi-surrealist approach.

McCullers's friend Truman Capote's first novel, a masterpiece of Southern Gothic, featured an ambiguous relationship between a sensitive boy and his eccentric, reclusive gay uncle. Signet's 1949 reprint featured the then popular Peephole motif, in the form of a broken window. At this peephole, the reader looks out rather than in - at a naked couple, almost unnecessarily tiny, in an Edenic scene. But it was Harold Halma's black & white photo of the author, sinuously reclining on a chaise longue and gazing invitingly at the reader from the back cover, that caught the public's attention. The notorious sybarite Denham Foutts, one-time boyfriend of arts patron Peter Watson, was so taken with the picture that he wrote Capote a blank cheque from Paris with the word "Come!" scrawled on it.

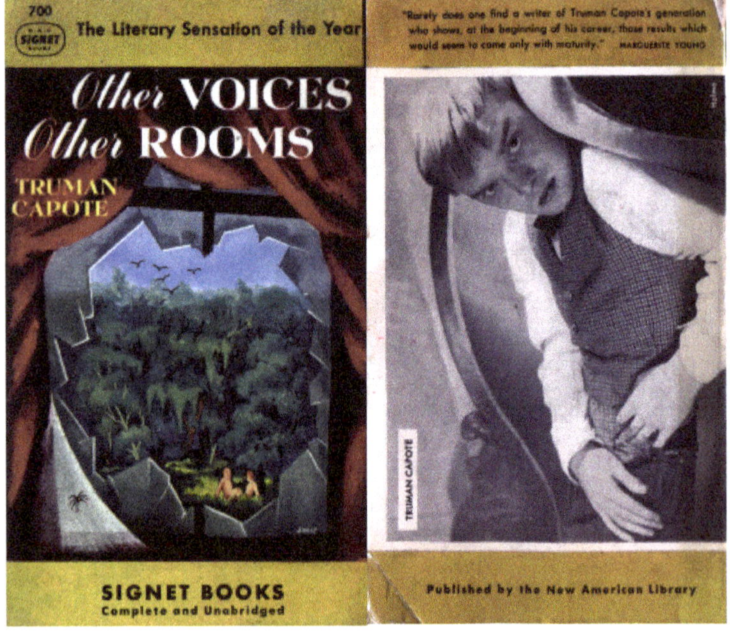

Truman Capote - *Other Voices, Other Rooms* (Signet, 1949) (front & back)

The Fifties

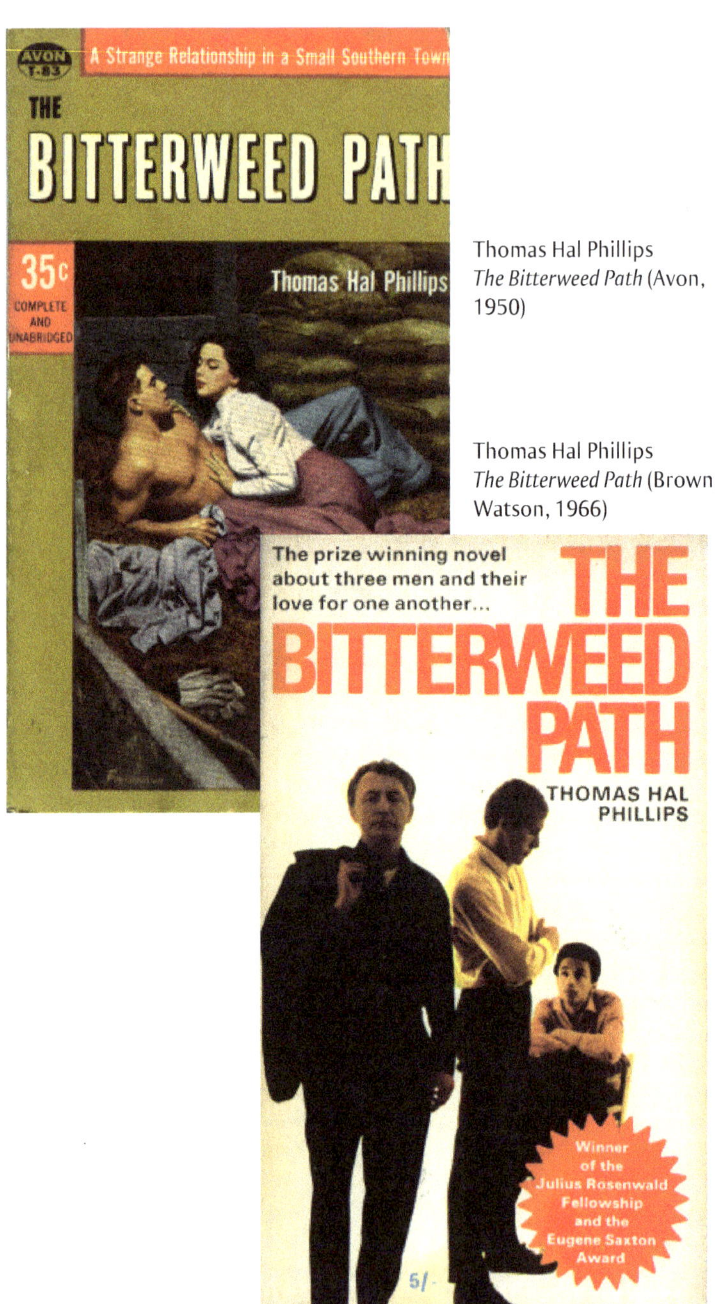

Thomas Hal Phillips
The Bitterweed Path (Avon, 1950)

Thomas Hal Phillips
The Bitterweed Path (Brown, Watson, 1966)

Set in the South, *The Bitterweed Path* charts the story of a young man's emotional and sensual involvement with a friend and his father. Avon's 1950 edition of this first novel by a young writer exemplifies one approach frequently taken in the early years of gay paperbacks by publishers seeking a wide readership. Though marriage and heterosexual relationships form a decidedly secondary plot element, they are emphasized in the cover painting by Gilbert Fullington. The only clues to gay subject-matter are the code word "strange" and the shirtless hunk's less than enthusiastic response to the woman's advances. The back cover is only slightly more revealing. On a British edition published sixteen years later, the text is more to the point and the woman has disappeared, though from the arrangement of the three models, it is difficult to guess what is supposed to be going on.

The publication of the first Kinsey Report and Gore Vidal's breakthrough gay novel *The City and the Pillar* in the same year delivered Post-War America a one-two punch. After an early success with his precocious war novel *Williwaw*, Vidal risked everything in publishing what was to become the most notorious gay novel of the post-war period. The *New York Times* refused to review it, or even accept advertising. Most reviews were hostile and Vidal wrote that he was "lectured firmly on the delights of heterosexual love." Even so, the book went through many paperback editions, with the author tinkering with the manuscript several times along the way, eventually rewriting the entire text. The original paperback shows a James Avati painting of a Concerned Woman in a strapless dress looking ambiguously at a Disconsolate Young Man. The back cover reveals the homosexual theme - and the handsome author. In the same publisher's redesigned edition five years later, the earlier cover illustration has been replaced by a scissors-and-paste fragment from the cover of another gay novel, Fritz Peters' *Finistère*. Only the Disconsolate Young Man remains, and "Personal tragedy" has become merely "a Lonely

Search." A British edition two decades later is more explicit, featuring a David Hockney drawing of two young men in bed together. An Afterword by the author tells a fascinating tale of the much rewritten novel and its rocky reception.

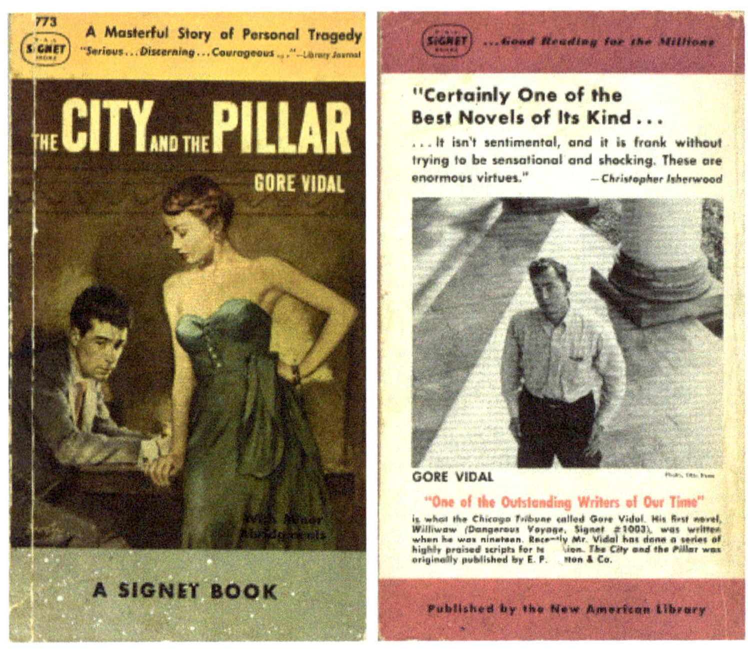

Gore Vidal - *The City and the Pillar* (Signet, 1950) (front & back)

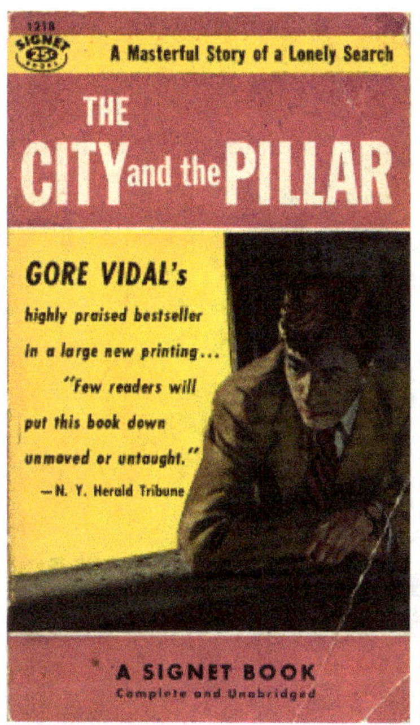

Gore Vidal
The City and the Pillar
(Signet, 1955)

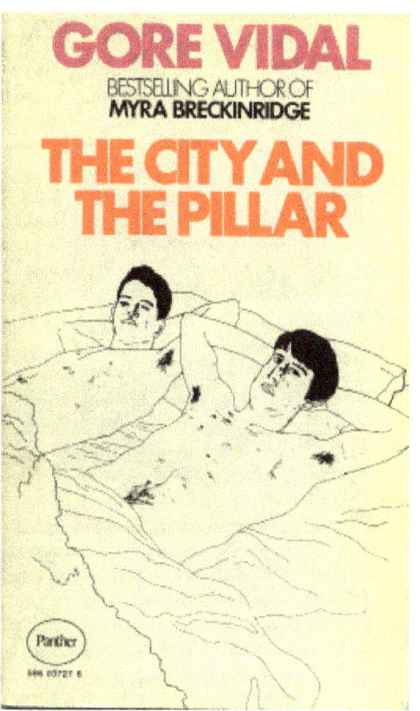

Gore Vidal
The City and the Pillar
(Panther, 1973)

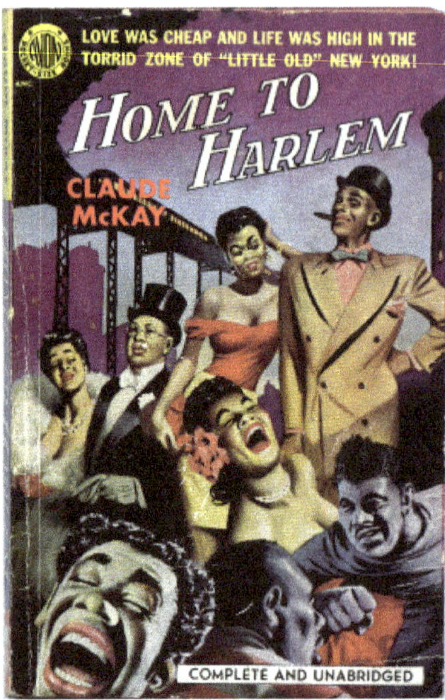

Claude McKay
Home to Harlem (Avon, 1951)

Many of the luminaries of the Harlem Renaissance were homosexual or bisexual, including Claude McKay, whose popular novel of Harlem life included some gay incidents ("The Good Times He Wanted He Could Only Find in Harlem!"). Avon issued its edition in tandem with Louis Sobol's collection of journalistic articles about Broadway society, *Along the Broadway Beat.* Both books bore the rich, distinctive cover art of Raymond Johnson. In spite of promising "Behind the Scenes of the Gay White Way," Sobol's inconsequential rubbernecking tour managed to ignore everything gay.

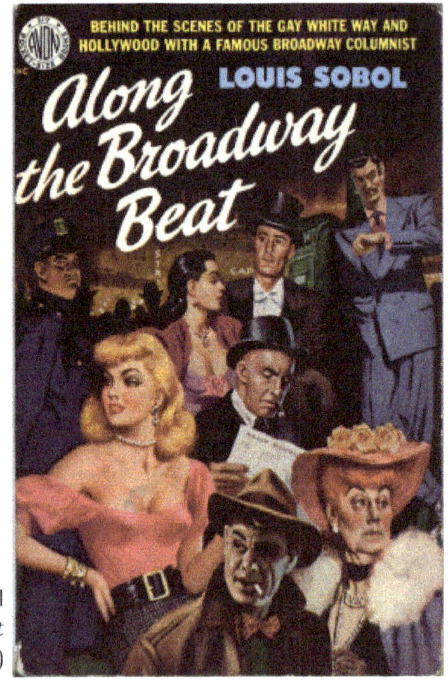

Louis Sobol
Along the Broadway Beat
(Avon, 1951)

Finistère was one of the breakthrough gay novels of the post-war period, though its tragic ending harkened back to earlier conventions. Signet's 1952 edition shows the frequently used Triangle motif, with the woman apparently oblivious to her partner's interest in yet another Disconsolate Young Man.

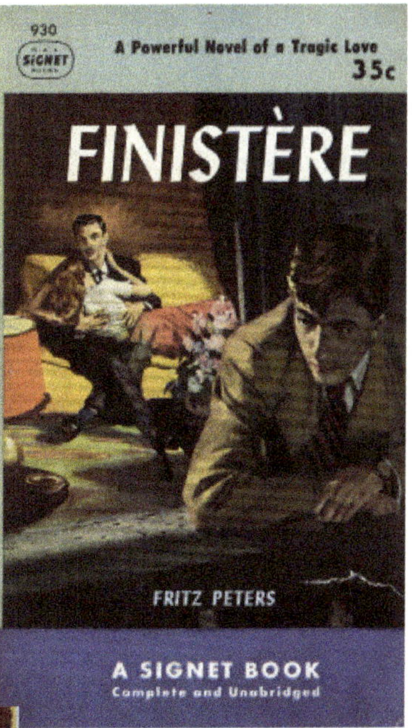

Fritz Peters
FinistPre (Signet, 1952)

The man on the cover of *Man Divided*, just as disconsolate, is regarded sceptically by a woman adjusting her clothing. Blurbs announce "the shadows (of) a twilight world," "a halfworld," and "an affair that was doomed from the start," contrasted to the "wholesome love" of heterosexuality. But the blurb beneath the picture ("a man's greatest tragedy - and fear") as well as the poses of the couple - particularly the man's hands - suggest impotence. Latent homosexuality as a cause of impotence with women

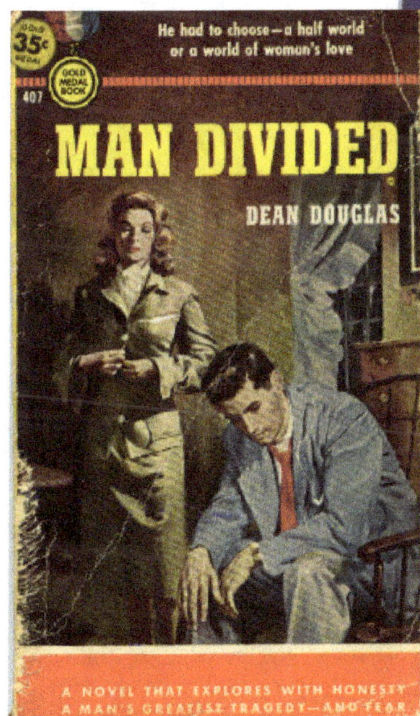

Dean Douglas
Man Divided (Fawcett Gold Medal, 1954)

surfaces as an underlying male fear in the postwar period.

One of the most popular British contributions to the emerging gay literature of the Fifties was *The Heart in Exile.* Written by émigré Hungarian psychiatrist Adam de Hegedus under a pseudonym, it gave readers a look at gay society as well as gay individuals. Lion Library's edition showed street cruising and a scene in a bar, as well as a psychiatric patient on the analyst's couch. The back cover shows a man with crooked fingers drawing a long, black coat around himself as he looks furtively over his shoulder. The blurb quotes *Time* magazine: "sordid facts and stunted lives..."

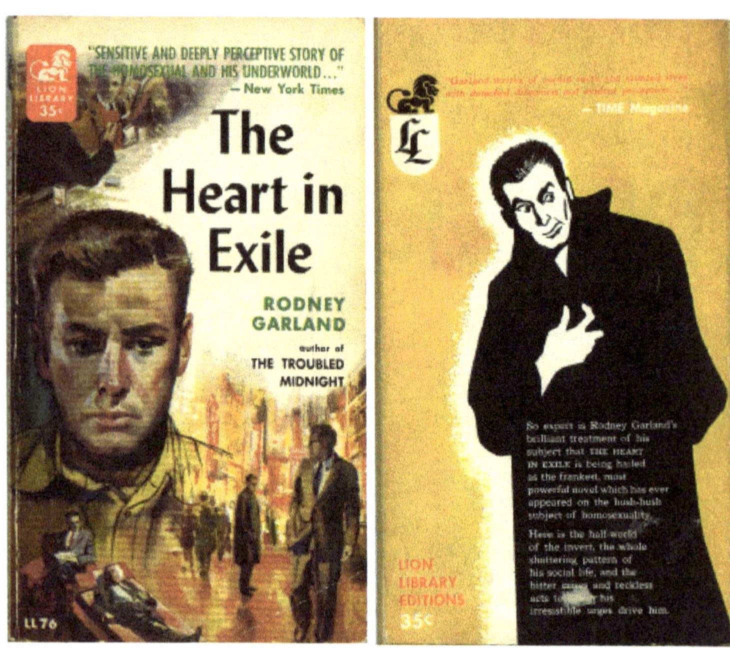

Rodney Garland
The Heart in Exile (Lion Library, 1956) (front & back)

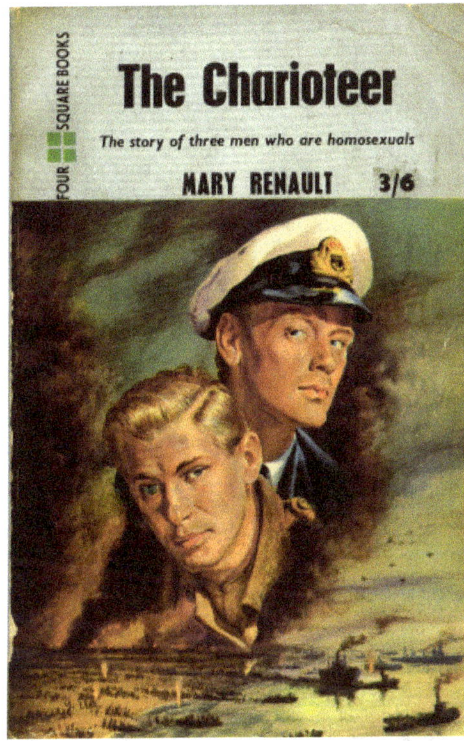

Mary Renault
The Charioteer
(Four Square, 1959)

Another key novel of the era was *The Charioteer*, by Mary Renault - one of a surprising number of women who wrote novels about gay men. The cover text is matter-of-fact: "The story of three men who are homosexuals." The painting indicates the World War II setting, the two men's gaze engaging the viewer.

Dyson Taylor's novel of a married man having a gay affair displays several motifs frequently used in the Fifties and Sixties - the Disconsolate Young Man with downcast gaze, the Concerned Woman (again, buxom and looking down at him) and the imperfectly defined male figure lurking or looming in the shadowed background, projecting an aura of menace. The triangle on Jay Vickery's *Gaydreams* published more than a decade later includes a similar Lurking Figure. The woman is trying hard to interest the young man - who may be waiting for someone else.

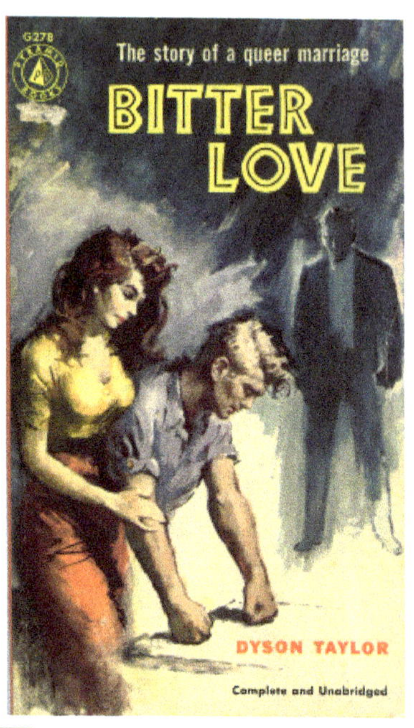

Dyson Taylor
Bitter Love (Pyramid, 1957)

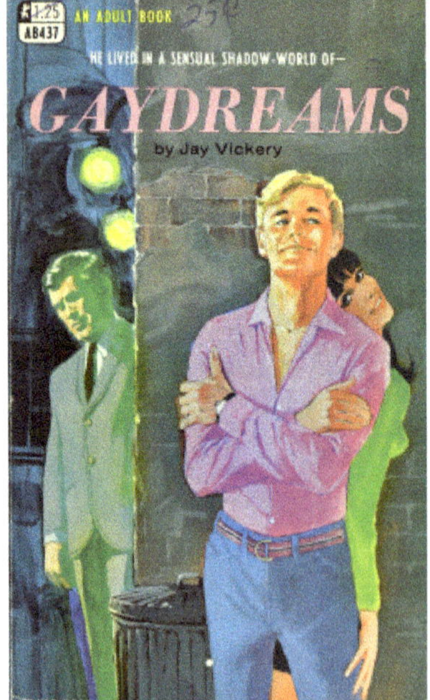

Jay Vickery
Gaydreams (Greenleaf Classics, 1968)

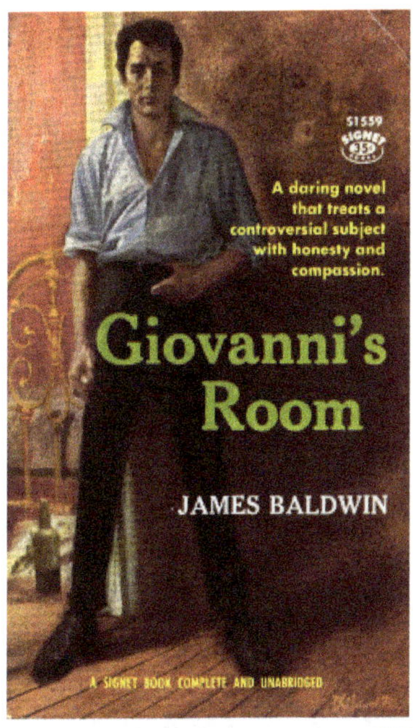

James Baldwin
Giovanni's Room (Signet, 1959)

An up and coming writer on the strength of his early work, black American novelist James Baldwin was warned against publishing this overtly gay novel, *Giovanni's Room* as it was felt it would harm his reputation. The original US paperback edition featured a richly rendered painting by Daniel Schwartz, one of the best illustrators of the day. Here, the cliché male predator lurking in the darkness has been brought into the light - and turns out to be tall, dark and handsome. A bed and a half-empty liquor bottle are suggestively included. Key words in the cover text such as "daring," "controversial" and "compassion" hint at gay subject matter. In a much later, British Corgi edition, the homosexual theme is explicitly stated, and illustrated by a tableau of two young men - one wearing only a towel, the other looking away.

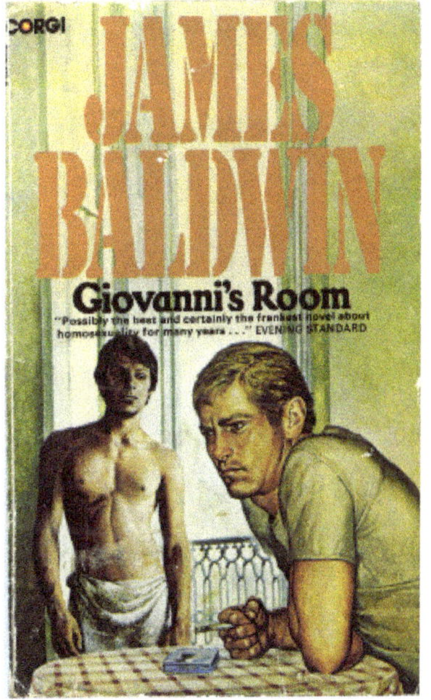

James Baldwin
Giovanni's Room (Corgi, 1977)

The Sixties

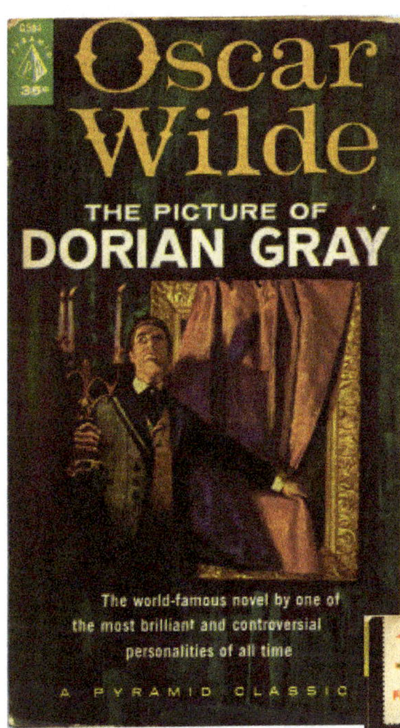

Oscar Wilde
The Picture of Dorian Gray
(Pyramid, 1961)

Wide paperback distribution brought the classics to new readers - and to a whole new class of readers. Pulp editions of books like Balzac's *Droll Stories,* gaudily adorned with busty babes, quickly became a publishing cliché. (On the other hand, the cover of an anonymous gay novel called *All the Sad Young Men* - "He was plunged into the half-world of homosexuality!" - displayed a full-colour detail of "The End of the World" by Luca Signorelli! It shows men in tight pants with codpieces.) From the Forties through the Nineties, classics with homoerotic content like Walt Whitman's *Leaves of Grass,* Oscar Wilde's *The Picture of Dorian Gray* and Thomas Mann's *Death in Venice* appeared in a succession of paperback editions. Wilde's martyrdom

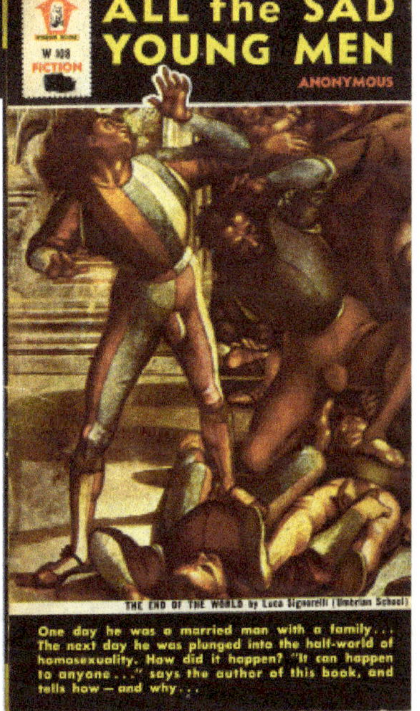

Anonymous
All the Sad Young Men
(Wisdom House Inc., 1962)

inevitably coloured the background to "Victim," a breakthrough film thriller about the destructive effects of the British anti-homosexual laws. Dirk Bogarde played a married man - ironically, a lawyer - who, afraid of emotional involvement, ignores a plea for help from a young man he has been seeing. When blackmailers drive the young man to suicide, the lawyer sets out to expose them. Corgi's movie tie-in

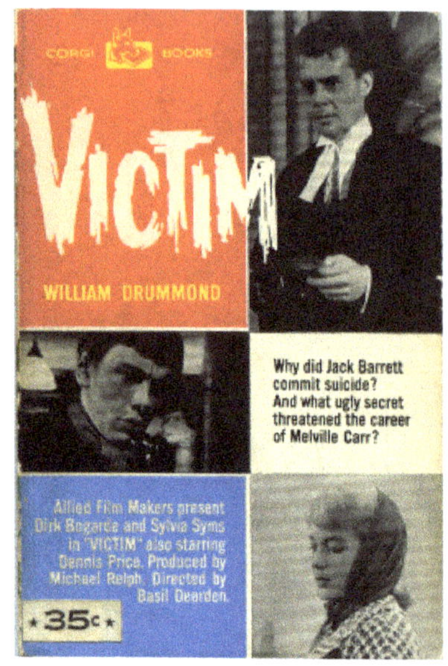

William Drummond
Victim (Corgi, 1961)

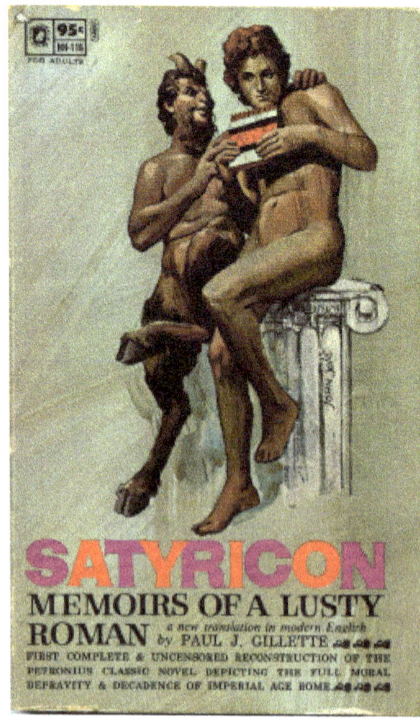

Petronius
Satyricon (Holloway House, 1965)

novelization recapitulated the traditional furtive Triangle - now disassembled into three isolated panels. Bogarde as the lawyer looks stunned; Peter McEnery as the young victim, trying to communicate, looks worried. Sylvia Sims as the Concerned Woman (wearing a demure headscarf) Looks Down. On the back cover, a kindly policeman offers the desperate youth a meal.

Probably the most reprinted of all the classics

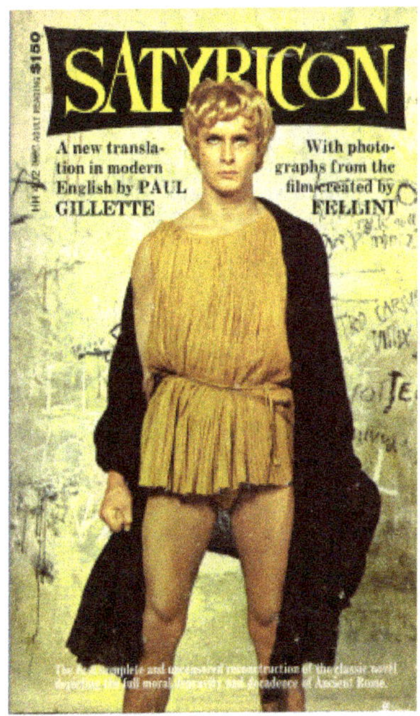

Petronius
Satyricon (Holloway House, 1970)

was the fragmentary Roman novel *The Satyricon*, with many US and British editions including an updated version entitled *Satyricon 70*. In one version, from a publisher of "Famous Erotic Classics," gay content is suggested by a naked young man being ogled by a satyr - an incident not to be found in the nonetheless relentlessly homosexual story. Five years later, a new edition appeared, augmented by black & white stills from Federico Fellini's recent film interpretation of the novel. This may have been an edition of dubious legitimacy as Ballantine published an official book of the screenplay, with lavish colour illustrations, the same year.

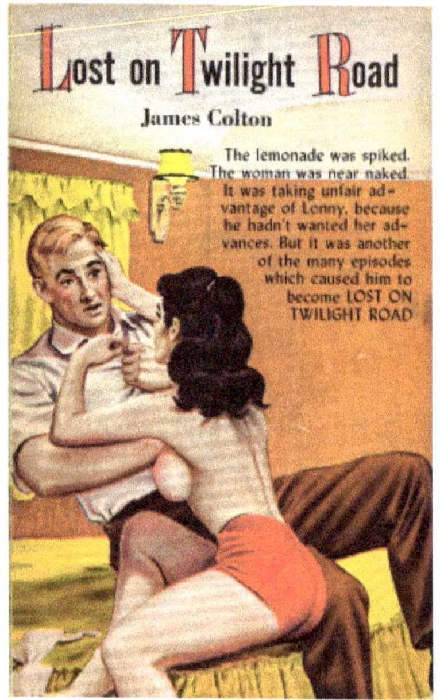

James Colton
Lost on Twilight Road
(National Library Books, 1964)

Lost on Twilight Road, an early pseudonymous novel by Joseph Hansen harks back to the gay-novel-in hetero-disguise motif more common in the '50's. The code word "twilight" and the stunned expression on the man's face as he fends off the busty babe's advances suggest the possibility of gay content; the back cover confirms it.

Lonnie Colman's surprisingly upbeat Sixties novel *Sam* was packaged was packaged to telegraph several strong hints: the code words "frank," "twilight" and "strange," the flamboyantly limp wrist, lavender background and ostentatious haberdashery. As with many editions of the day, once the browser reveals his interest by turning the book over, the back cover blurb confirms his suspicions: "The story of a successful man who is also an unashamed homosexual." At the other end of the spectrum from the

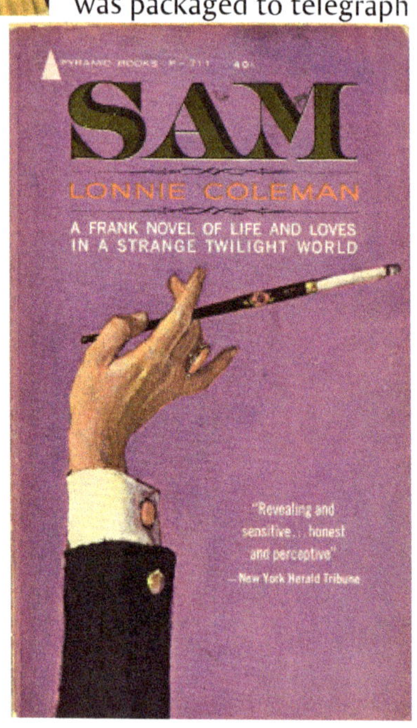

Lonnie Coleman
Sam (Pyramid, 1962)

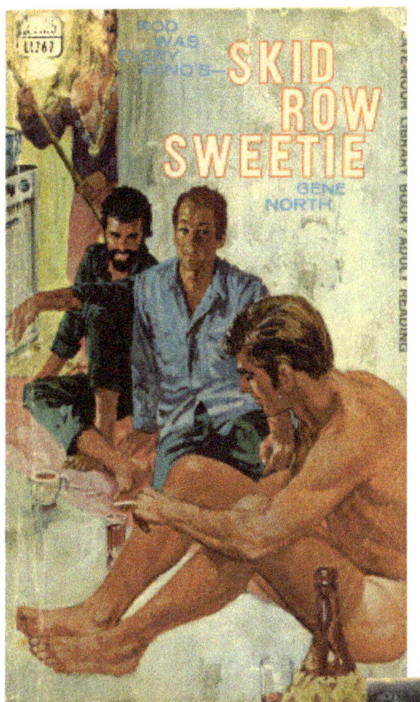

Gene North
Skid Row Sweetie
(Late-Hour Library, 1968)

over-dressed professional man in *Sam*, a novel by Gene North, *Skid Row Sweetie*, shows a naked young man entertaining two relatively well-groomed down-and-outs while an androgynous figure stands in the background. The blurb announces "Rod was every wino's Skid Row Sweetie," It is beginning to be apparent that "we are everywhere."

Softcover Library's paperback original edition of Sean O'Shea's *Whisper* displays a cover motif common in the Fifties and early Sixties: one man looks at another who looks away-at the reader, at a woman, or into space. Homoeroticism was assumed to be predatory rather than reciprocal. Later in the Sixties, as attitudes began to change, the motif changed with them, the second man turning to meet the gay gaze.

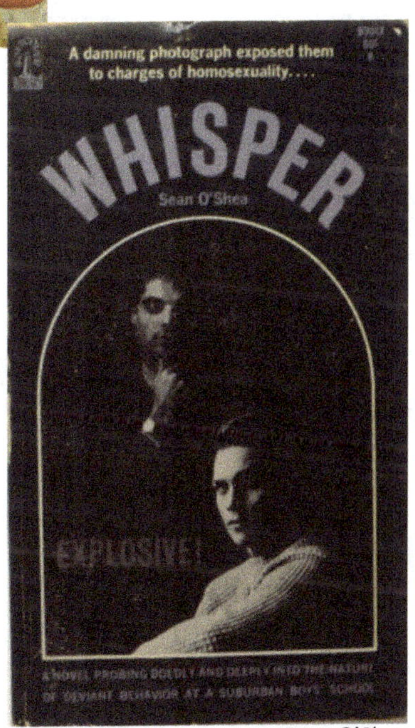

Sean O'Shea
Whisper (Softcover Library, 1965)

The Solitary Young Man was the simplest, and one of the most frequent, gay cover motifs. In Harry J. Schaare's cover for the Pyramid edition of *The Divided Path,* lavender is the predominant colour. Grove's reprint of John Rechy's bestselling *City of Night* dispensed with the lavender, showing an appropriately gritty urban nightscape, again with a solitary figure, in

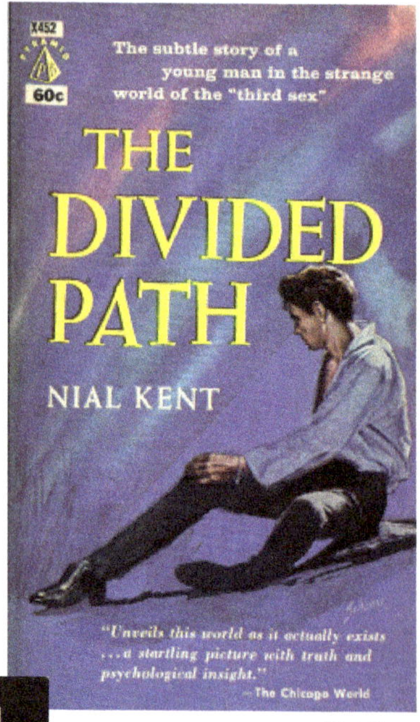

Nial Kent
The Divided Path (Pyramid, 1964)

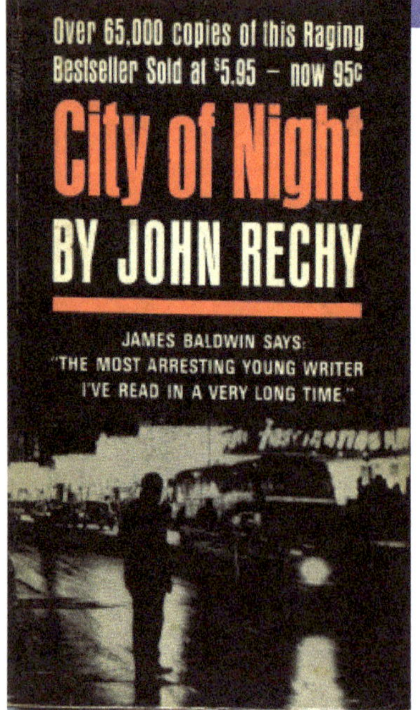

John Rechy
City of Night (Grove Press, 1964)

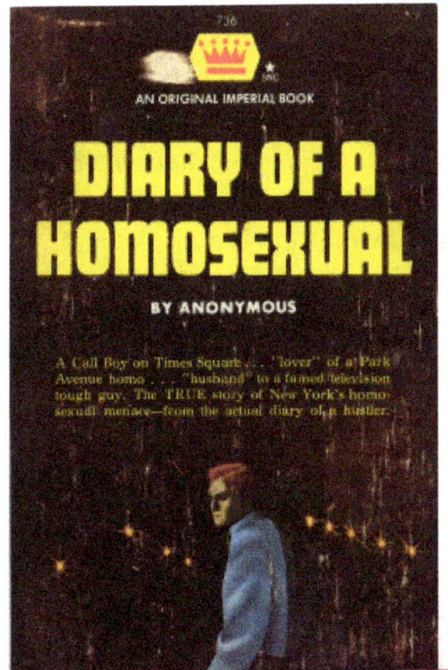

Anonymous
Diary of a Homosexual
(Imperial, 1965)

an image that may have influenced Imperial's cover of the anonymous *Diary of a Homosexual*, also about a hustler and published the following year. *City of Night*'s back cover blurb promises "tawdry... deviate" goings-on. For W.D. Angel's *10 Bad Boys*, the porn publisher 101 Enterprises employed a striking, if slightly blurred, photographic approach.

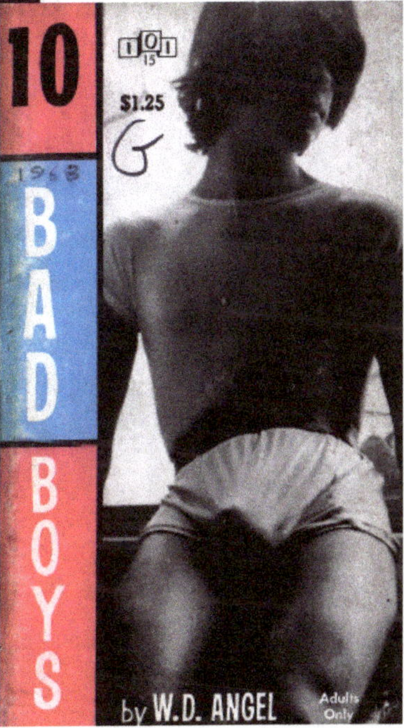

W.D. Angel
10 Bad Boys
(101 Enterprises, 1968)

In the 1960's, a number of sensationalistic, quasi-exposés on "the twilight world" began to appear, usually with titles like *America's Homosexual Underground* or *The Homosexual Generation. Sex Behavior of the Homosexual* promises chapters on "Bohemian Sex Cults," "The He-Man Homosexual" and "Phallic Worship." The cover shows a solitary man in leotards and flip-flops. *The Other Men* clothes a version of Michelangelo's David - long a gay icon - in a psychedelic Sixties outfit. *Confessions of a Married Man* employs the much-used Triangle motif, with a blurb describing bisexuality as a "twisted, confused, perverted... aberration." One early nonfiction book on homosexuality was entitled *They Walk in Shadow*, and shadows and silhouettes remained frequent illustrative devices.

Lucius B. Steiner
Sex Behavior of the Homosexual (Genell, 1964)

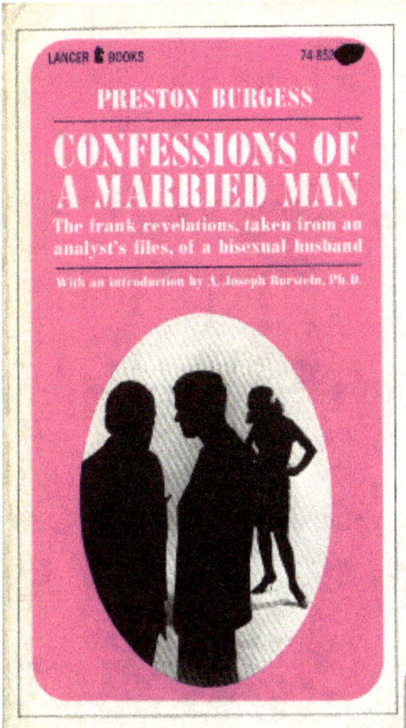

Preston Burgess
Confessions of a Married Man
(Lancer, 1966)

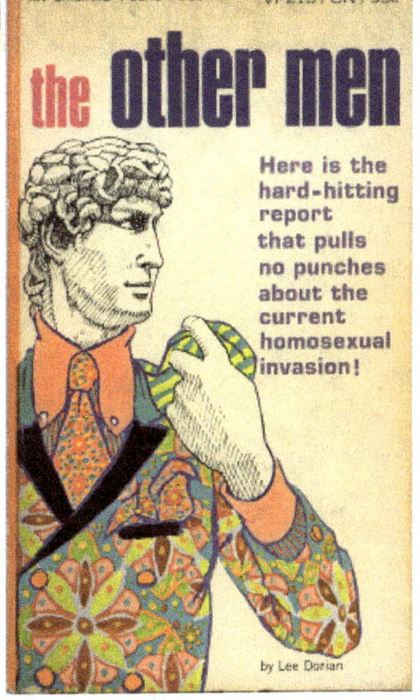

Lee Dorian
The Other Men
(Viceroy Books, 1966)

By the mid-1960's, the earlier reticence about discussing homosexuality was falling away, homophile organizations were becoming more visible and young gays were starting to organize on college campuses. The years 1965-6 saw a spate of paperback novels from Lancer, Paperback Library and several other publishers showing pairs

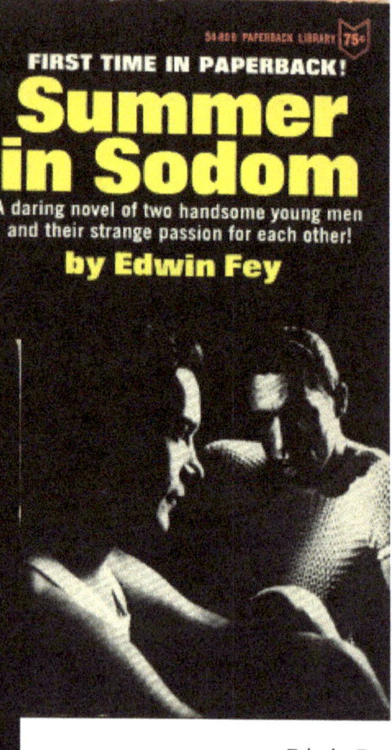

Edwin Fey
Summer in Sodom
(Paperback Library, 1965)

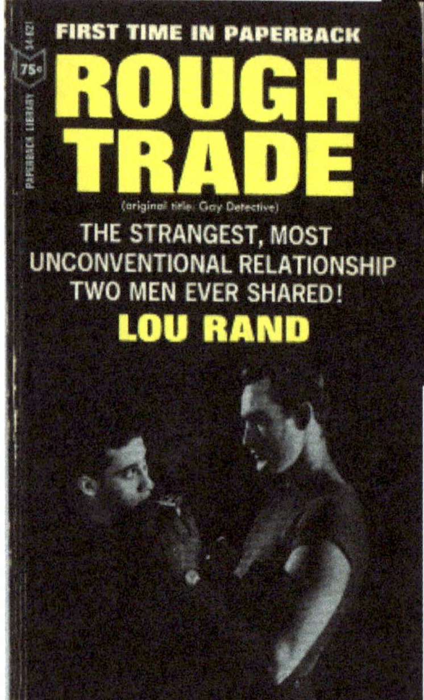

Lou Rand
Rough Trade
(Paperback Library, 1965)

of men, lit in high contrast from the front or side, and posed against black backgrounds, as though emerging from darkness. The covers also show a slight but significant shift from the Looking Away motif common in the past. *Strange Marriage* shows a Cruising motif: one man looks at the other who turns as if to return the gaze. Lou Rand's *Rough Trade* (a reprint of *Gay Detective*) is even bolder, showing two men face to face as one lights the other's cigarette. Unlike the similar cigarette-lighting scene on Signet's 1949 edition of Charles Jackson's *The Fall of Valor,* there is no woman to look suspiciously from the foreground. James Barr's *Quatrefoil,* which dealt with naval personnel, was originally published by the small New York firm of Greenberg and took fifteen years to come out in paperback, in the US by Paperback Library and in an identical Canadian edition by Swan Publishing Co. in Toronto. The blurb is straightforward - "love between two men."

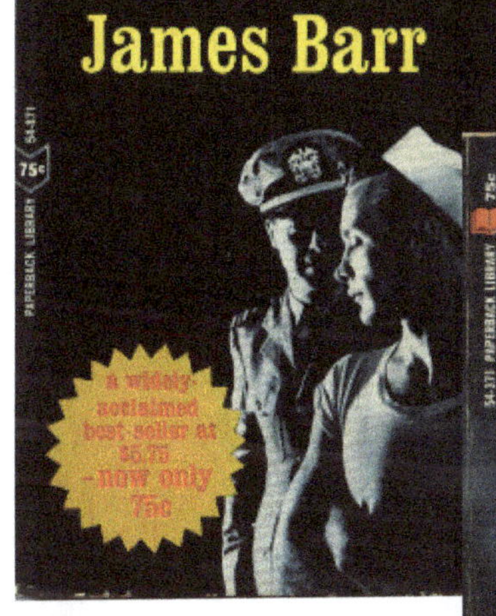

James Barr
Quatrefoil
(Paperback Library, 1965)

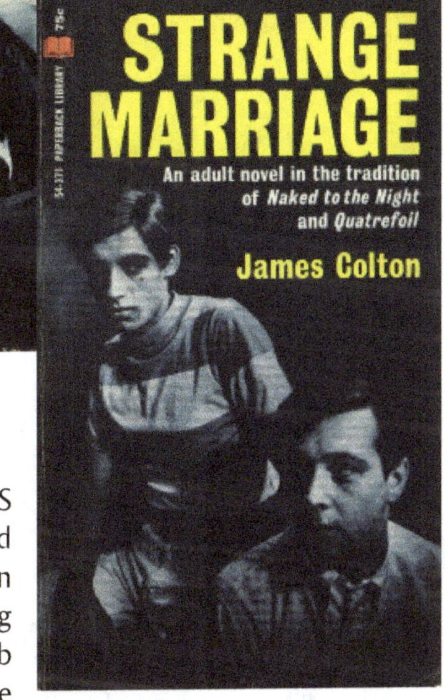

James Colton
Strange Marriage
(Paperback Library, 1966)

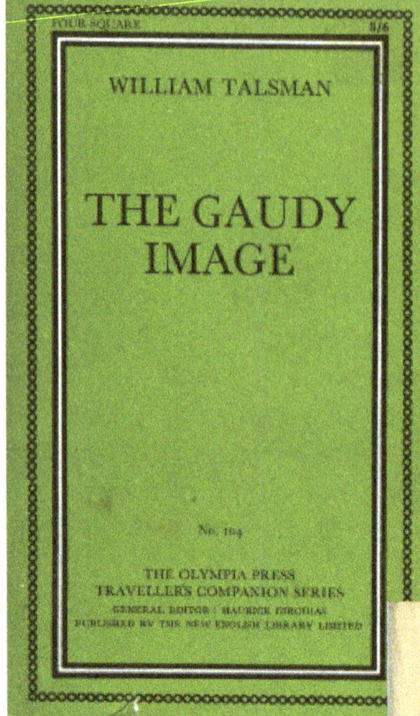

William Talsman
The Gaudy Image
(Olympia Press Traveller's Companion Series, 1966)

While *Quatrefoil* had a modest but respectable publishing history in hardcover, the novels by Fey, Rand and Colton/ Hansen were out-&-out pulp fiction, published as paperback originals. Their presentation, in spite of the predominace of black, was by the standards of the time more shocking than sombre.

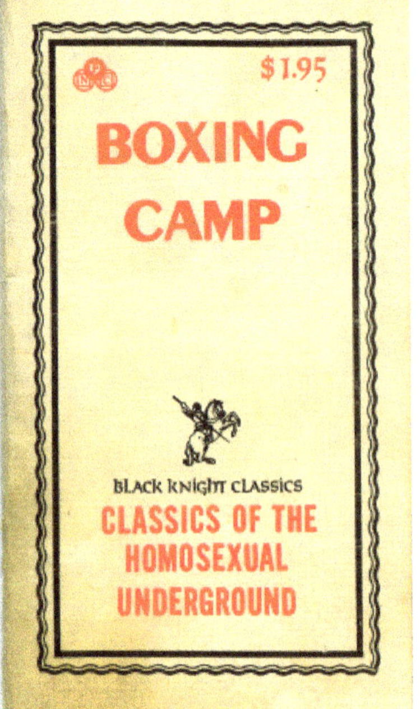

Anonymous
Boxing Camp
(Guild Press Black Knight Classics, 1969)

Perhaps surprisingly, some titles published by "porn houses" achieved an elegant restraint. For the originally French-based Olympia/Traveller's Companion, owned by the renowned Maurice Girodias, the lack of cover art originated in the need to avoid attracting undue attention from North American customs agents. For Guild Press, owned by the eccentric entrepreneur

Dr. Herman Lynn Womack (who for a time ran his business from the sanctuary of a psychiatric hospital), it sidestepped the problem and expense of commissioning cover art. Over the years, a surprisingly large number of gay paperbacks were issued with only lettering on the cover. For *The Gay Haunt*, Olympia spiced up its traditional green cover with an oval version of the Keyhole motif.

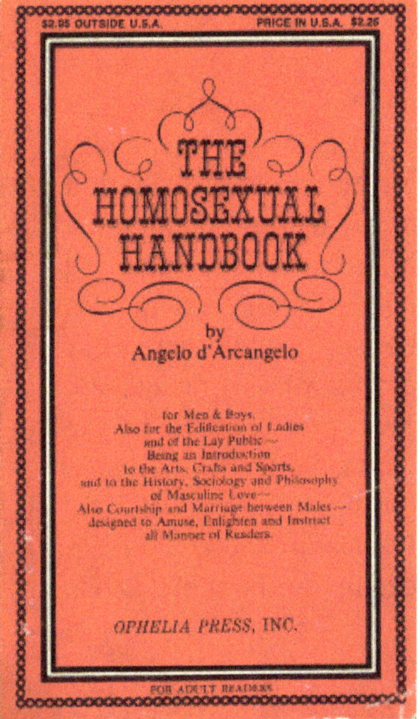

Angelo d'Arcangelo
The Homosexual Handbook
(Traveller's Companion, 1968)

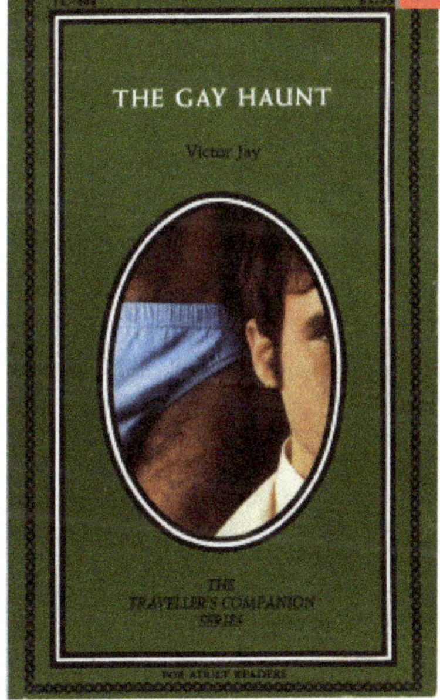

Victor Jay
The Gay Haunt
(Traveller's Companion, 1970)

By the 1960's, a series of precedent-setting legal cases had opened the way for the freer distribution of gay writing and pictorial representation, and a number of companies began publishing gay erotica of varying quality. Two books issued in the old-fashioned Digest format, *Queen of the Road* and *The Gay Rebels,* exemplify the more garish of the productions. Among the most popular pulps of the day were Richard Amory's "Loon" series, historical erotic fantasies about Indians and white men living and loving together in a pastoral early America. The leading gay porn publisher of the Sixties, Greenleaf Classics, issued the first of the books with a charming wrap-around cover painting showing an interracial pair in a benign outdoor setting. Several publishers issued novels featuring red/

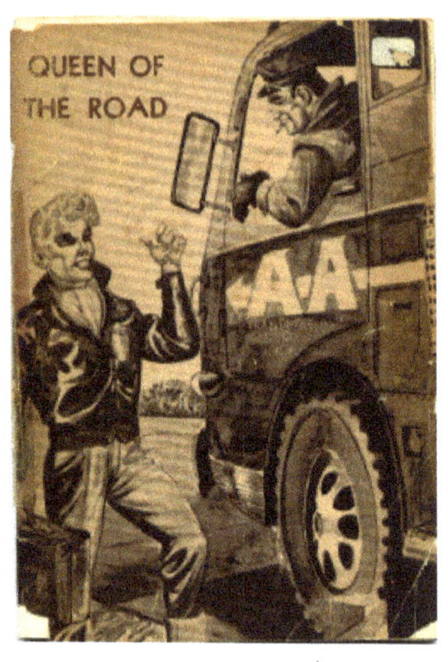

Anonymous
Queen of the Road
(Guild Press, 1966)

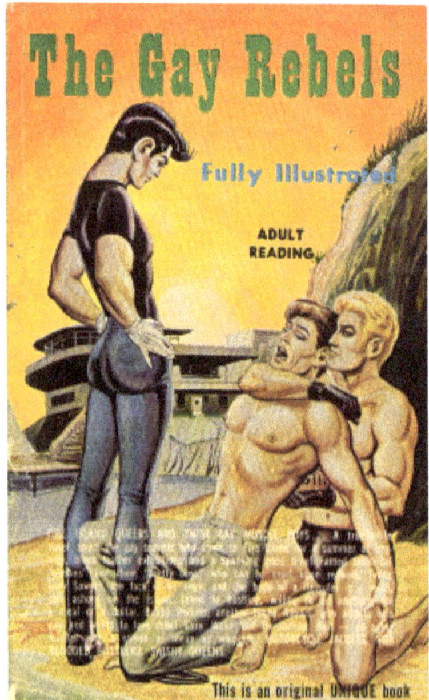

Larry Price
The Gay Rebels
(Unique, 1966)

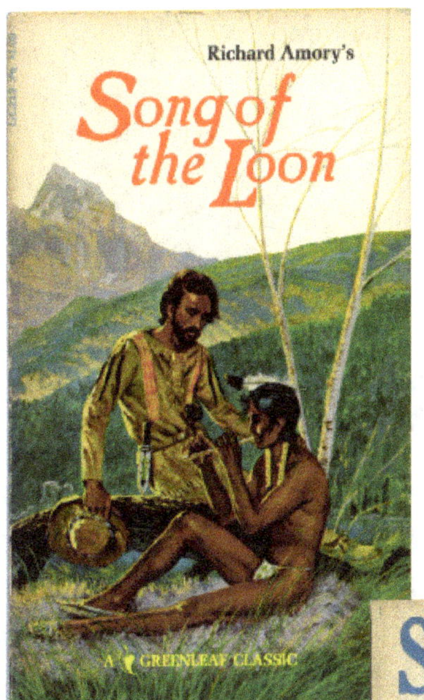

Richard Amory
Song of the Loon
(Greenleaf Classics, 1966)

white male pairs as cover motifs - including *Sky Eyes* by Carl Corley, an author who usually provided his own cover art. (Black/white pairs were fairly rare and other pairings almost nonexistent). The Loon series was so popular that Greenleaf issued a parody, *Fruit of the Loon*, showing two Indians, a buckskin-clad white man and a goose. The back cover showed madcap goings-on among pots of bear grease and chicken fat at the Circle 69 Ranch. The rather plain cover of Jeff Lawton's *Truck Stop* opened to reveal a combination of explicitly homoerotic writing and textual experimentation including graffiti-like graphics and concrete poetry.

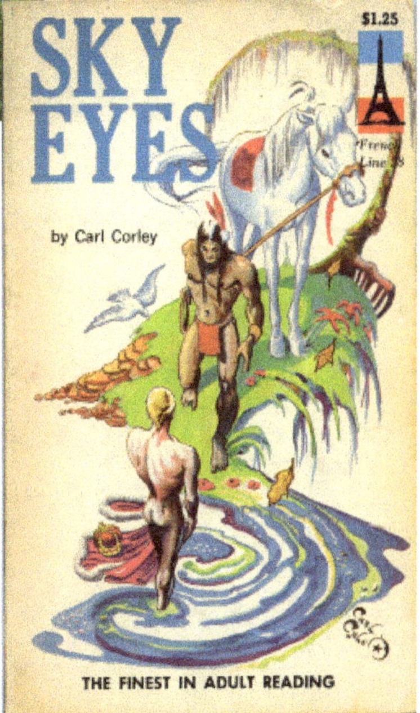

Carl Corley
Sky Eyes
(Publisher's Export Co.
French Line, 1967)

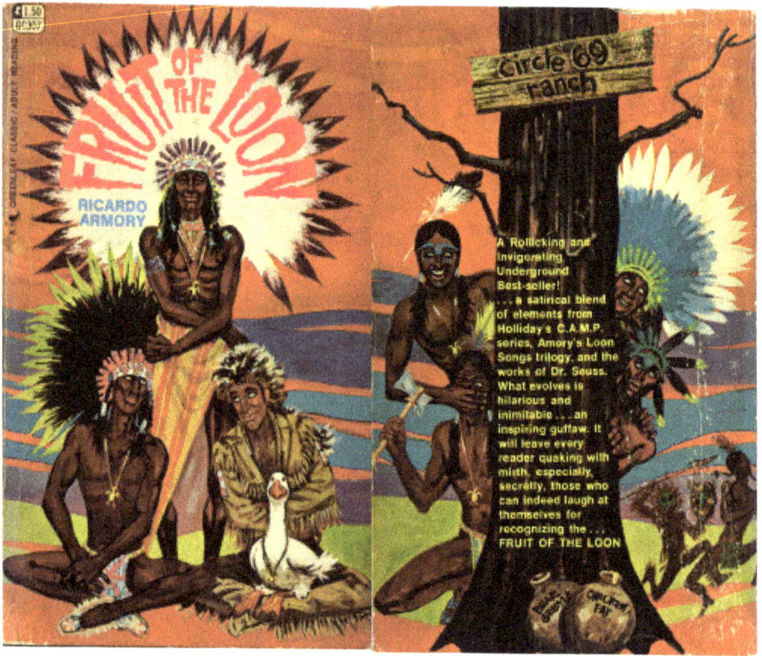

Ricardo Armory. *Fruit of the Loon* (Greenleaf Classics, 1968) (front & back)

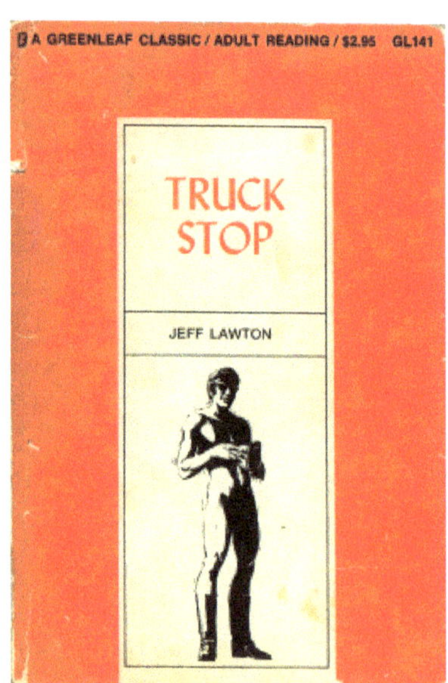

Jeff Lawton
Truck Stop
(Greenleaf Classics, 1969)

As openly erotic gay novels began to circulate widely, publishers of literary fiction took the hint. The half-naked hunk became a frequent, surefire motif - enticing, yet not too explicit. A wide range of literary fiction from

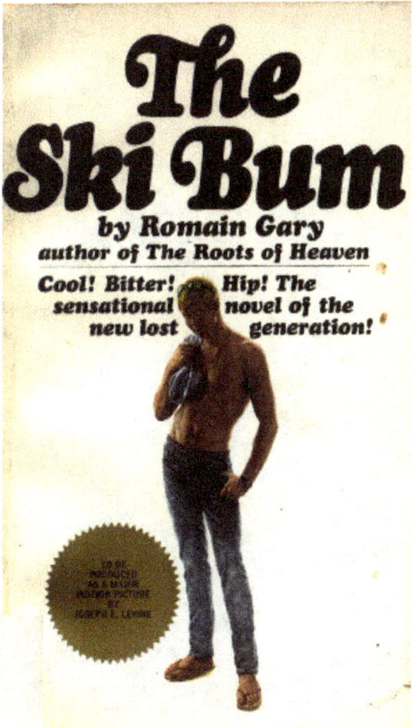

Romain Gary
The Ski Bum
(Bantam, 1966)

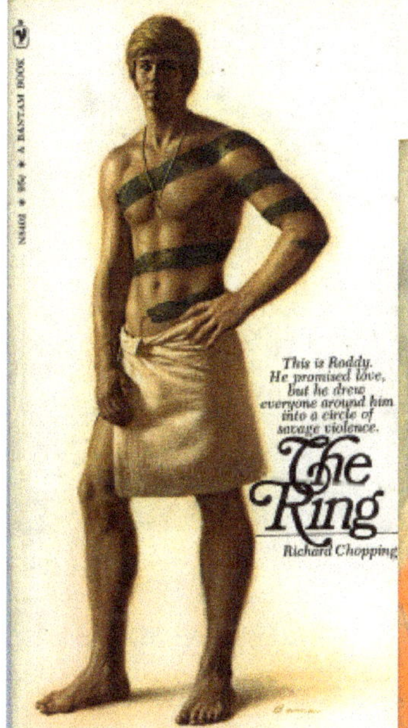

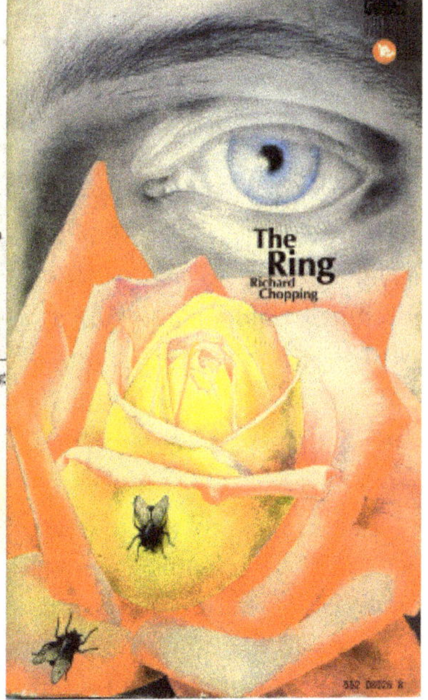

Richard Chopping
The Ring
(Corgi, 1968)

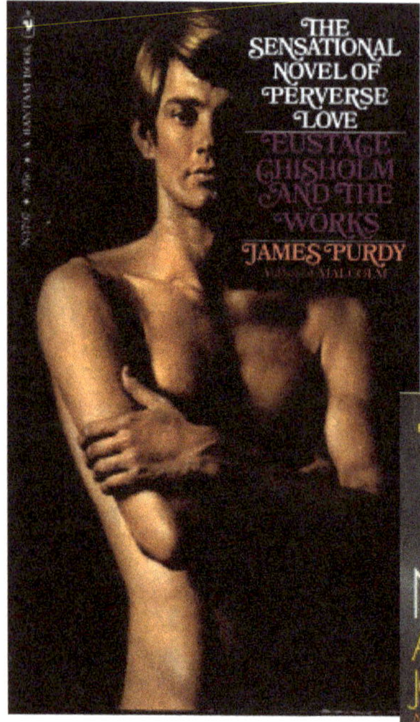

James Purdy
Eustace Chisholm and the Works (Bantam 1968)

1966 to 1970 shows covers with male nudes of semi-nudes. Though Romain Gary's *The Ski Bum* has no gay content, the painting of a beautiful shirtless young man was presumably designed for broad appeal. For Richard Chopping's *The Ring*, the same publisher commissioned James Bama, one of the most accomplished paperback cover artists, to paint the fetching, towel-clad youth with the snake tattoo. The novel's British edition displayed an equally striking cover painting by the author.

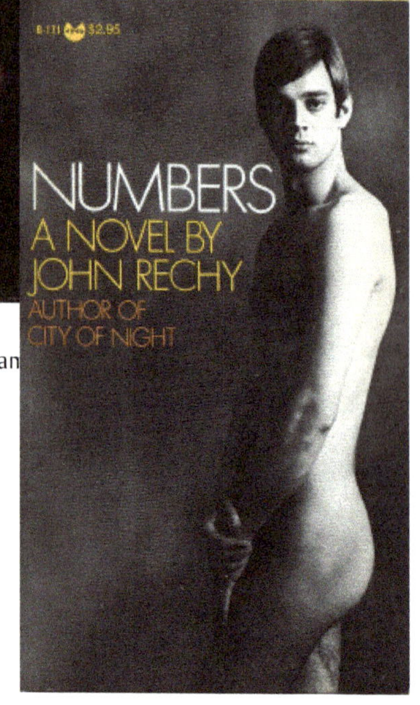

John Rechy
Numbers
(Grove Evergreen Black Cat, 1968)

Bama also provided cover art for *The Lieutenant*, a novel about a homosexual incident among US marines. He provided a double focus for the reader's attention with his rendering of a winsome, shirtless youth and a purposeful-looking older martinet - separated by text about a "web of shame." The phrase harks back to the coded language of earlier times: "shame" as a code word for male homosexuality was first publicized by Lord Alfred Douglas' 1892 poem "Two Loves" in which a homosexual youth (or youthful spirit) is denied the right to call himself "Love" and is called "Shame" instead; he replies, "Have thy will;/ I am the love that dare not speak its name." The "love that dare not speak its name" entered the language (largely displacing "the abominable crime not to be mentioned among Christians") and "Shame" began to appear as a code word in poems by Aleister Crowley and others. In the Eighties, "Shame" was transformed into its opposite, "Pride."

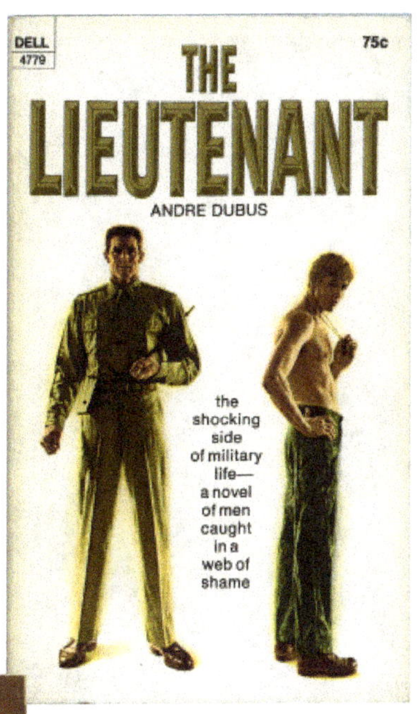

Andre Dubus
The Lieutenant
(Dell, 1968)

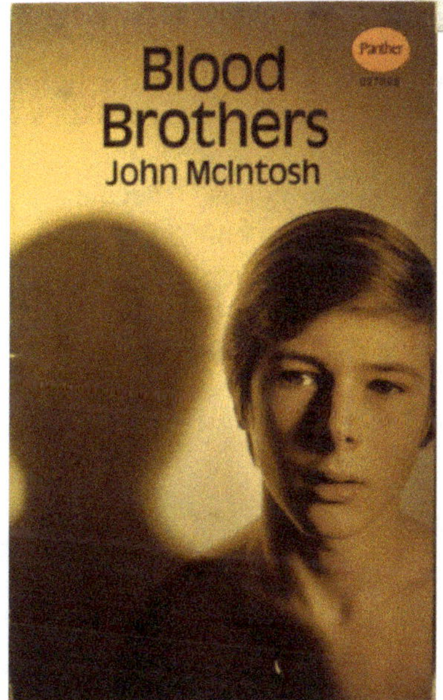

John McIntosh
Blood Brothers
(Panther, 1969)

Blurbs on the James Purdy and Angus Stewart novels, "Perverse Love" and

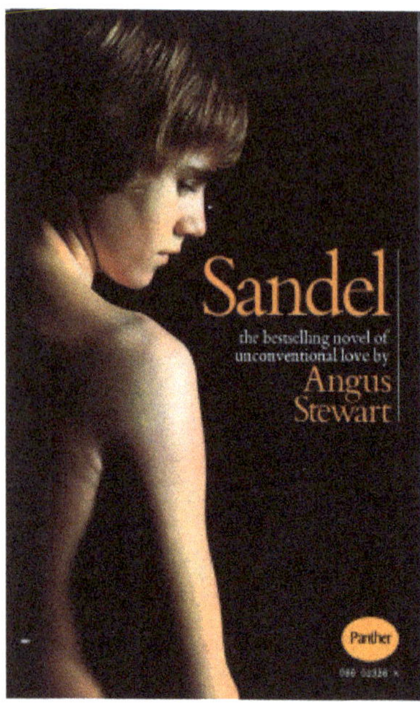

Angus Stewart
Sandel
(Panther, 1970)

"Unconventional Love," offer additional clues to their subject matter, while John Rechy is prominently identified as the author of his best-known gay novel. John McIntosh's *Blood Brothers*, set in South Africa with an interracial theme, relies on the complex suggestions of the Shadow motif to suggest the contents. Though explicit homosex could now be depicted, interracial romance could still only be hinted at.

The high gloss, white backgrounds that began to appear on some late Sixties paperbacks lasted through the Seventies, becoming as emblematic as the black backgrounds of only a few years earlier. Homosexuality was emerging from the shadows into the glaring daylight.

In the late Twentieth century, paperback editions of translated European fiction – from the classic *Death in Venice* to Alberto Moravia's *Two Adolescents* and the postmodern *The Lost Boy* – found readers all over North America. Both these Panther editions of European novels employ the double exposure approach to suggest their subject matter. Roger Peyrefitte, the author of the classic schoolboy novel *Special Friendships*, though a diplomat, was also a highly cultured provocateur: the boys in his book are considerably younger than the cover models depicting them.

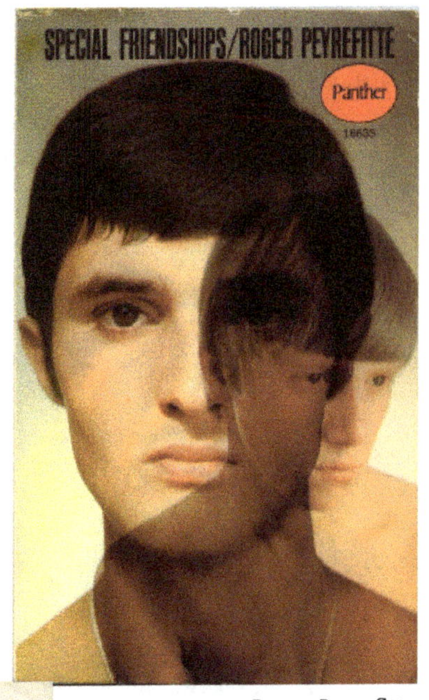

Roger Peyrefitte
Special Friendships
(Panther, 1968)

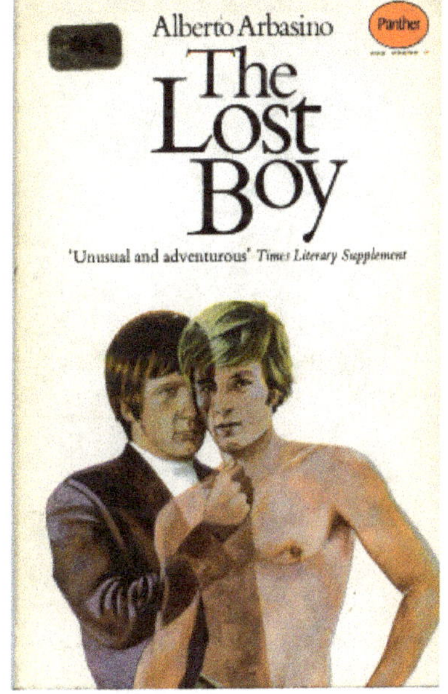

Alberto Arbasino
The Lost Boy
(Panther, 1970)

In the countercultural 1960's small gay groups began to sprout up on American college campuses. Then, in the summer of 1969, the Stonewall riots in new York City changed the rules of the game. Gay Liberation and the Manson Family were the last Sixties protests and both turned violent at the end of the decade. Yet the Gay Lib movement that developed through the early Seventies was utterly nonviolent and strongly influenced by Sixties hippiedom.

Dick Dale
The Price of Pansies
(Phenix Late-Hour Library, 1968)

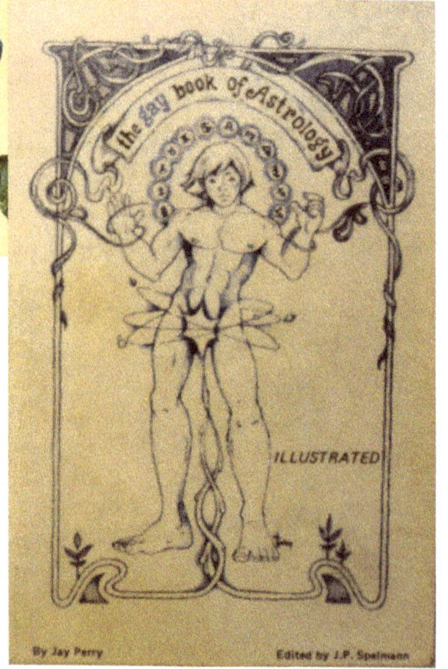

Jay Perry
The Gay Book of Astrology
(Big Ernie Enterprises, 1971)

Underground gay artists like Ralph Hall, Keith Haring and Sidney Smith developed aspects of the psychedelic aesthetic. A book of astrology for gay men featured drawings by Toby, a popular illustrator of the period, whose babyfaced characters suggested eroticized cupids in hippie attire, harking back - for it is already 1971 - to the Summer of Love. By contrast, a more established publisher of porn's attempt at a hippie book failed miserably. Though the blurb on Dick Dale's *The Price of Pansies* promises "He was a gay flower child!" the text is about a bisexual romp and the flower child is depicted as a clean-cut youth in sunglasses and white sneakers with a pansy in his fly and a FOR SALE sign.

The Seventies

As the new decade approached, the Gay Liberation Movement and *The Boys in the Band* gave America yet another unexpected one-two punch that it could not duck. Mart Crowley's wicked drawing-room drama, first a play, then a movie, hit just as the old rules were being ditched. As if for the first time, the old, self-hating, middle-class faggotry

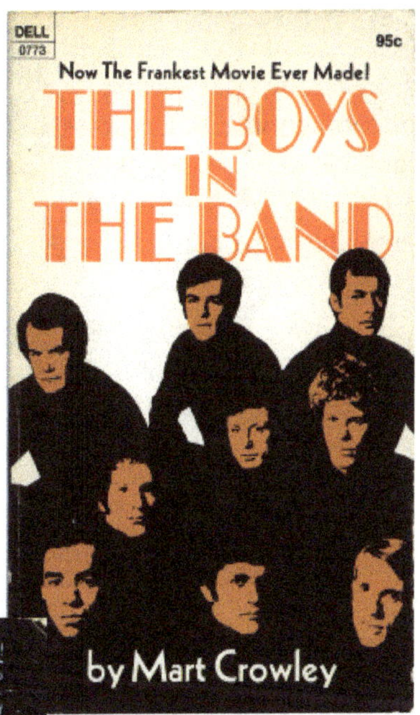

Mart Crowley
The Boys in the Band
(Dell, 1970)

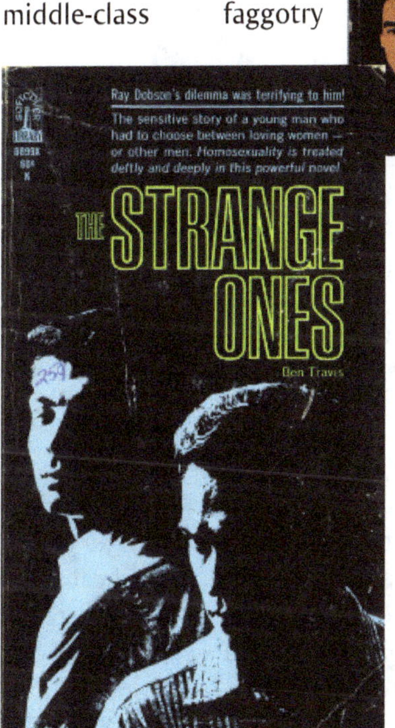

Ben Travis
The Strange Ones
(Softcover Library, 1965)

was examined and found wanting. The cover of the 1970 movie tie-in combines the black, out-of-the shadows background of the old Sixties editions with the white background favoured in the Seventies, all-revealing if slightly clinical. The similar faces of the nine characters in the cast peer from identical black outfits, or rather, from an undifferentiated black mass, perhaps anticipating the "clone" phenomenon that was just ahead. "The Frankest Movie Ever Made!" announces the blurb.

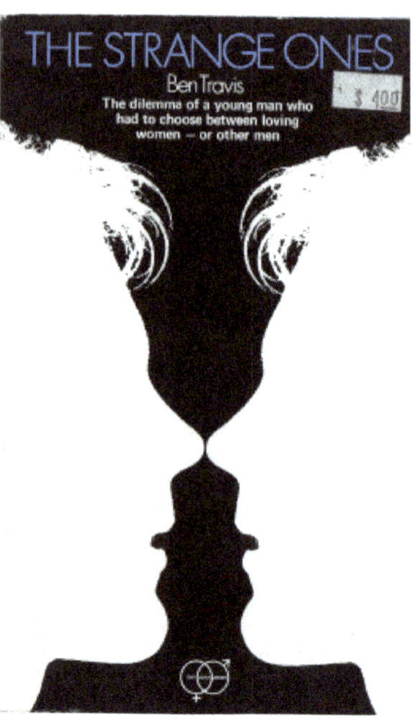

Ben Travis
The Strange Ones
(Softcover Library, 1970)

Black and white contrast was also employed in the 1970 edition of Ben Travis's *The Strange Ones.* An edition from the mid-Sixties had used the black background, half-lit faces and Looking Away motif common at the time. The new decade demanded a new look, and a stylish twin silhouette was chosen - not, apparently, of two men, but of one man turned to face himself. He appears to like what he sees.

Panther's edition of Laurence Eben's *Shadow Game* used a different kind of black and white contrast to suggest the tortuous difficulties of an interracial gay relationship in apartheid-era South Africa. Here, as with *Blood Brothers*, published by the same company five years earlier, the shadow metaphor is prominent. But the shadows no longer stand for all homosexuality, as in the past, but specifically for homosexuality between black and white. The cover shows two men, one black, one white, stripped to the waist, but *both* looking away - and even *turning* away - from one another. Here, the shadows and Looking Away motifs of earlier years linger into the mid-Seventies, displaced to another country and reinforced by the ambiguities of race and racism. "The

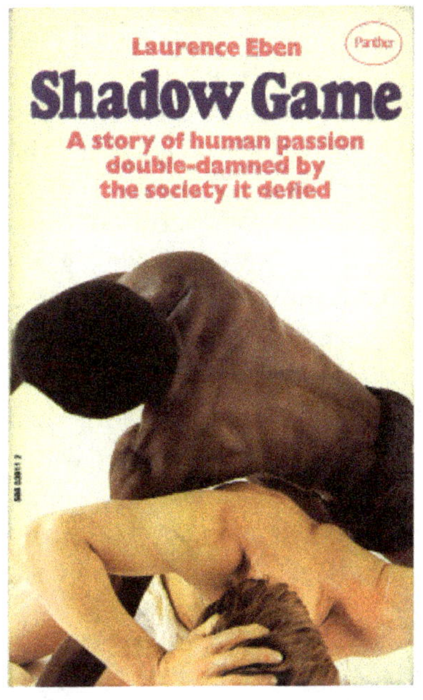

Laurence Eben
Shadow Game
(Panther, 1974)

stakes," reads the blurb (it could be 1950) "were scandal, despair and death..."

Gordon Merrick began his career in the late 1940's with such novels as *The Strumpet Wind* and *The Demon of Noon.* Though fairly well received, they did not achieve great popular or critical success and Merrick disappeared from the literary scene for almost a quarter of a century. He returned with a vengeance in 1970 with an overtly gay novel, *The Lord Won't Mind.* In its paperback incarnation, *The Lord Won't Mind* and its various sequels - romantic fantasies about rich, handsome, well-endowed men - became gay best-sellers, partly due to the distinctive, breakthrough cover art of Avon illustrator Victor Gadino. The cover of *The Lord Won't Mind* dispenses utterly with the Solitaries, Looming Presences and Looking Away conventions of the past. Here, the two handsome blond men

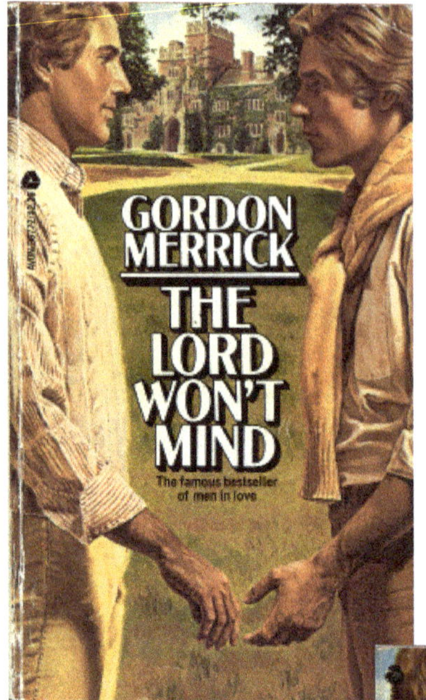

Gordon Merrick
The Lord Won't Mind
(Avon, 1971)

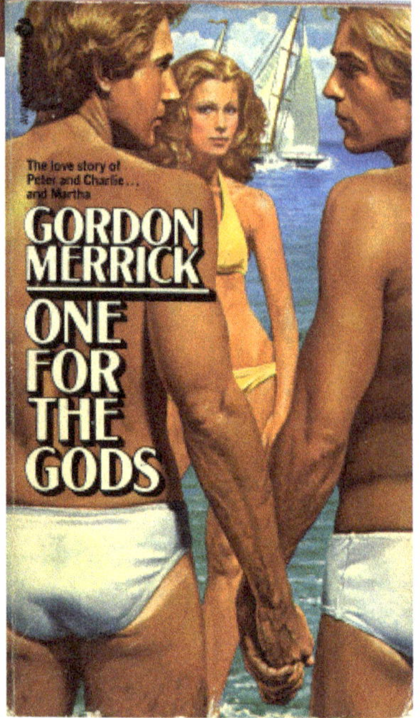

Gordon Merrick
One for the Gods
(Avon, 1972)

depicted are face to face, reaching out to one another while the sunlit, ivy-covered Princeton building in the background suggests opulence and respectability. The blurb reads simply "The famous bestseller of men in love." *One for the Gods* reprises the two-men-&-a-woman Triangle. As with Signet's 1949 edition of *The Fall of Valor*, everyone is dressed for the beach, but here, the men have already paired, and are holding hands, and the woman looks more knowing and less concerned. Several of Avon's Merrick books made clever use of wrap-around cover art. *An Idol for Others* shows a man in a business suit with a younger, shirtless man seen from behind. The reader cannot see their faces until the book is turned over. There, the men look at one another, one accepting the other's embrace.

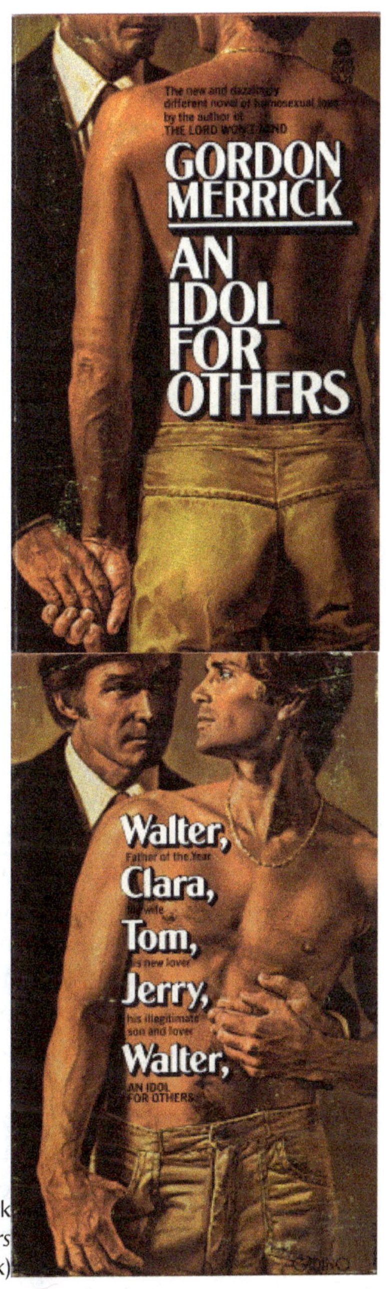

Gordon Merrick
An Idol for Others
(Avon, 1977) (front & back)

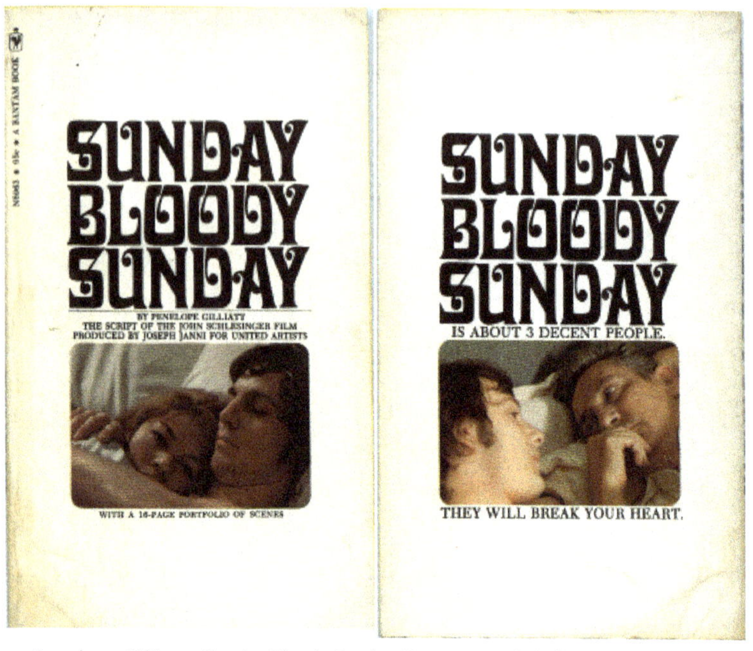

Penelope Gilliatt - *Sunday Bloody Sunday* (Bantam, 1971) (front & back)

In 1973, the American Psychiatric Association, under intense pressure from the Gay Liberation movement and increasing dissent from among its own members, removed homosexuality from its list of psychiatric disorders. Though many psychiatrists clung to their lucrative old opinions, they were rendered increasingly irrelevant by the changing public perceptions reflected in popular films and TV shows. Penelope Gilliatt's subtle screenplay and John Schlesinger's bold direction made "Sunday Bloody Sunday" one of the key films of the 1970's. A professional woman and a middle-aged physician are both involved with the same bisexual young artist. The scene in which the two men greet each other with a passionate kiss drew gasps from many cinema audiences. This edition of the script shows the hetero pair on the front cover, the gay pair on the back. Both couples appear intimate, yet neither seems completely comfortable, and the front cover retains a touch of the troubled or concerned woman motif of the past. But the back cover reassures the reader that "Sunday Bloody Sunday is about 3 decent people..."

By the 1970's, gay themes were also beginning to show up, albeit tentatively, on TV. *That Certain Summer* is a paperback original novelization of a teleplay about a teenager who discovers his father is gay. The two men (played by heterosexual liberals Hal Holbrook and Martin Sheen) look at one another; the son stands between them. The back cover describes the movie as "a milestone in TV history." The trend toward Problem Pictures continued into the next decade. *Making Love* is a novelization of a feature film billed as "a love story for the 80s." The two-men-and-a- woman Triangle is reprised - but here, though the woman is placed between the two men, the three engage the reader together, all smiles.

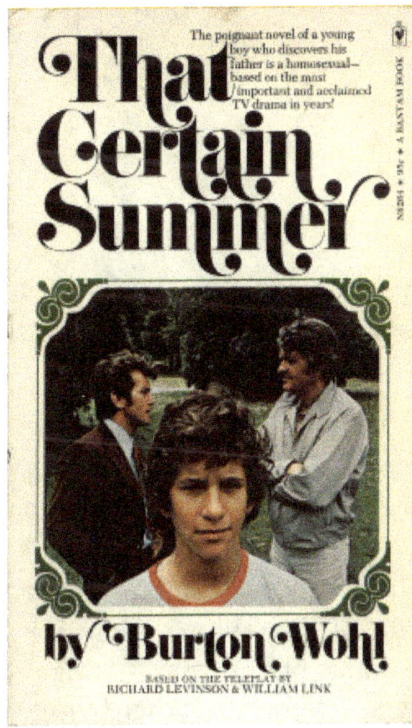

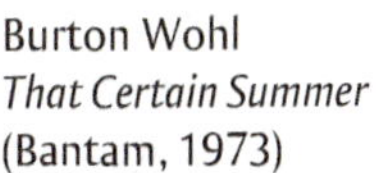

Burton Wohl
That Certain Summer
(Bantam, 1973)

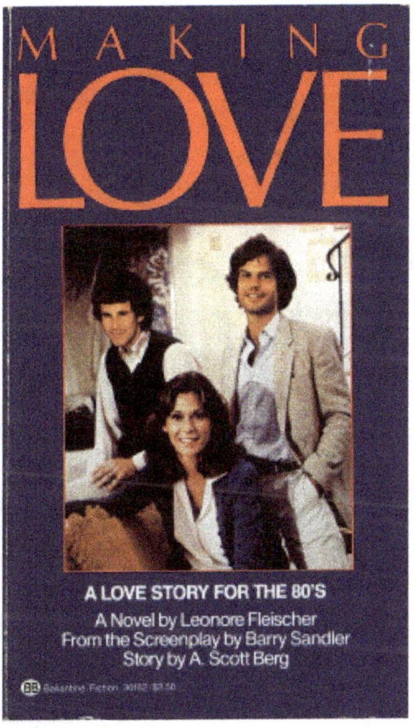

Leonore Fleischer
Making Love
(Ballantine, 1982)

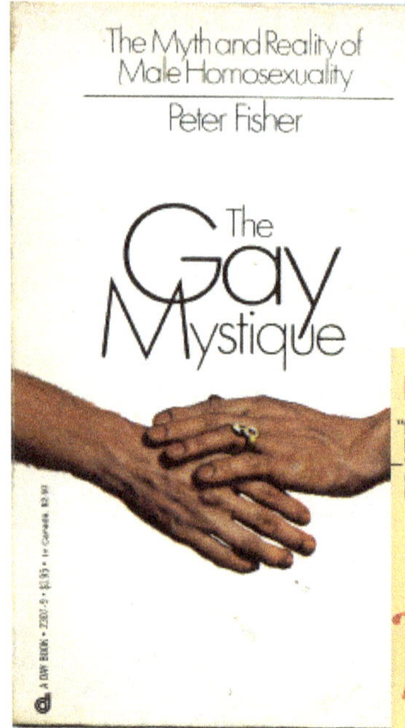

Peter Fisher
The Gay Mystique
(Day Books, 1978)

One of the first - and best - of the nonfiction books of the Gay Lib period, Pete Fisher's 1972 essay, *The Gay Mystique,* subtitled *The Myth and Reality of Male Homosexuality*, shows two male hands (one wearing a male symbol ring) reaching for one another, reminiscent of *The Lord Won't Mind* several years earlier. A moving passage in the book tells of the author's private marriage to his lover on the steps of a church. A contrasting approach was taken for Robin Lloyd's exposé-cum-rubbernecking tour of boy prostitution *For Money or Love*. Ballantine's censorious blurbs ("devastating... shattering...alarming") - one by a senator, the other by the prosecutor of the Manson Family - suggest deviant horror but the senatorial introduction reassures the reader of the book's respectability. The come-hither cover photo of a pretty boy in a leather jacket indicates the *real* content and readership.

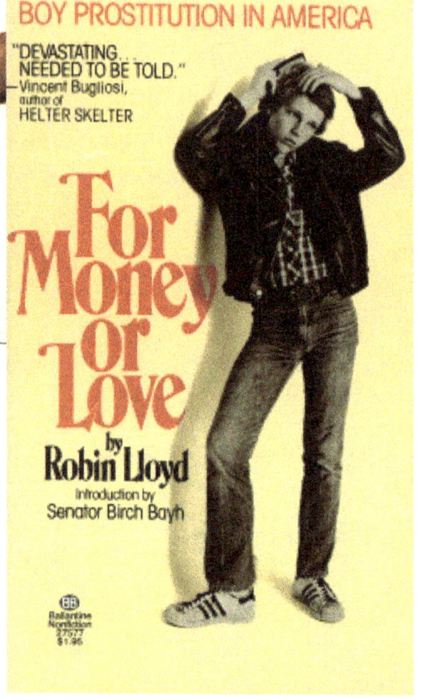

Robin Lloyd
For Money Or Love
(Ballantine, 1977)

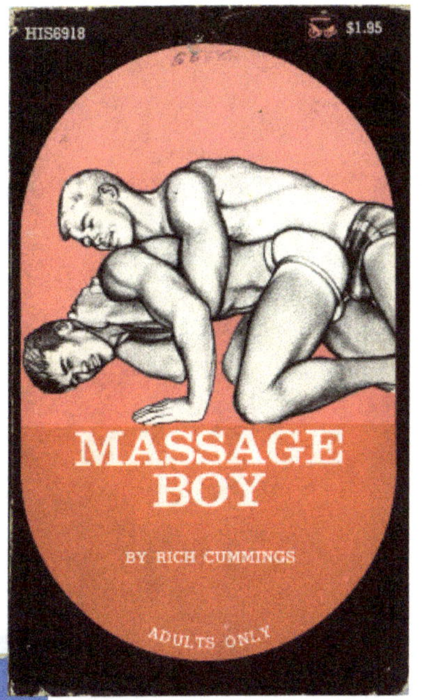

Novels from four different porno houses prominent in the 1970's show a variety of illustrative approaches. *Massage Boy* shows all-American jocks. One of a series of novels by "John Ironstone" (Frederick W. La Cava), *I Am Proud to Be Gay, Now I Want to Be Free,* employs a rare political motif - an urban streetscape with a burning car, Gay Lib banners and a sign suggesting orange juice pitch-woman Anita Bryant, then beginning her anti-gay rampage. The back cover quotes a prose poem about love by Walter Rinder. Ward Michaels' novel *Jonny Silver* shows a hitchhiking youth with a pattern of automobiles behind him suggestive of a snake with its tongue out. *Cycle Sadist* shows a rough customer in an emblematic leather jacket. His frontal nudity is nonetheless

Rich Cummings
Massage Boy
(Surrey House, 1972)

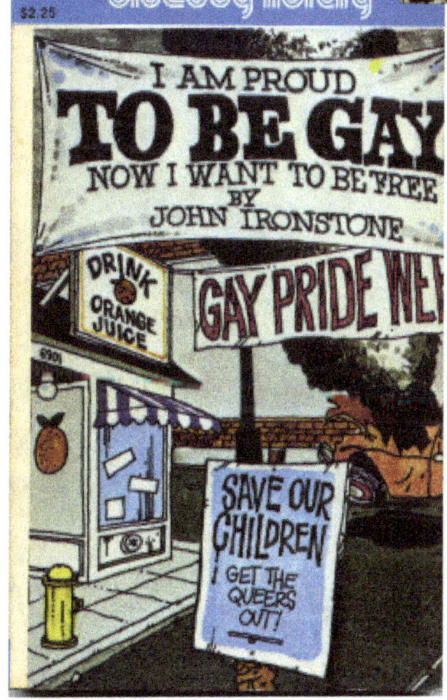

John Ironstone
To Be Gay
(The Blueboy Library, 1977)

discreet enough for some paperback racks.

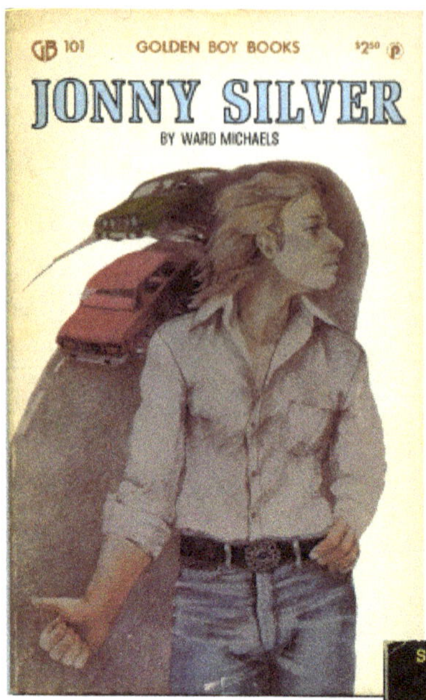

Ward Michaels
Jonny Silver
(Arena Publications Golden Boy Books, 1978)

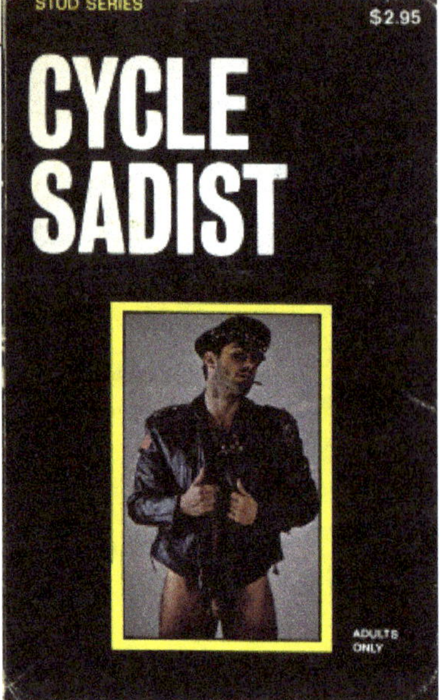

Jim Browne
Cycle Sadist
(Star Distributors Stud Series, 1979

The Eighties

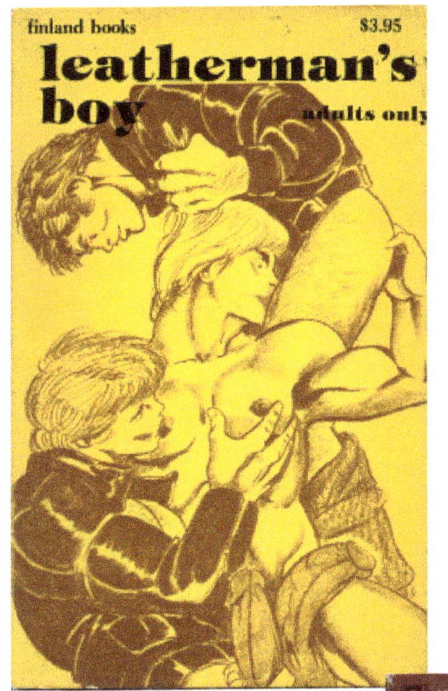

By the 1970's and '80's covers of porn novels were becoming more explicit. The iconic male threesome on *Leatherman's Boy* is a far cry from the old two-men-and-a-woman Triangle of the past. The publisher, Star Distributors, launched its Finland Books line to benefit from the widening popularity of erotic artist "Tom of Finland" (Tuoko Laaksonen) whose distinctive style Star's cover art evoked with modest success.

Anonymous
Leatherman's Boy
(Star Distributors Finland Books, 1983)

Other porn covers merely seemed explicit. On Jon Riggles' *Leather Sucker*, what at first glance appears to be a penis is actually the handle of a whip. Pictorial ambiguity was not the only deceptive feature; as with many porn novels, the title and cover illustration were assigned with little attention to content. The

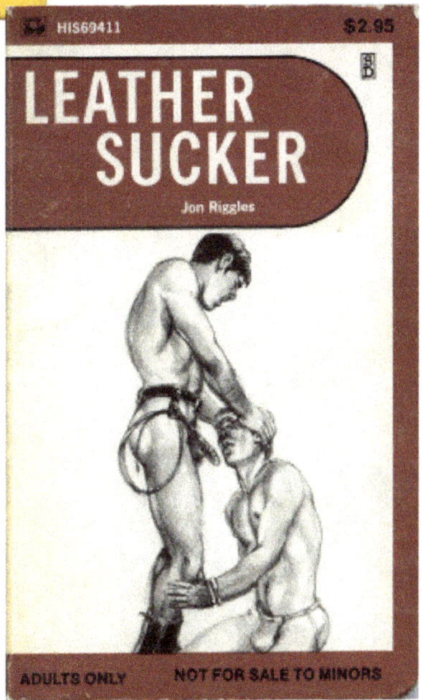

Jon Riggles
Leather Sucker
(Surree Ltd., 1980)

story, about a man who likes his partners to beat him up, says little about either leather or sucking.

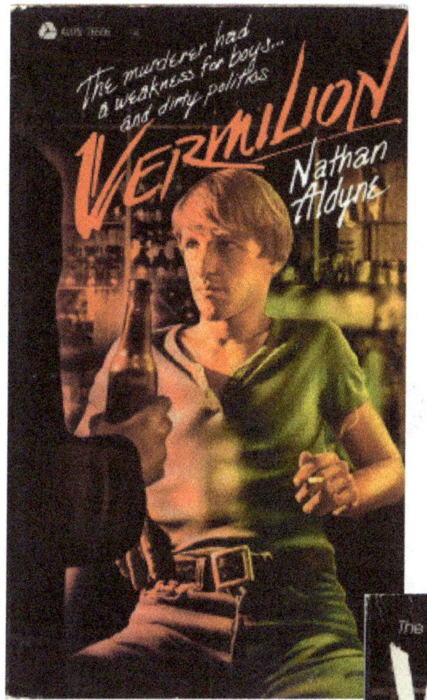

Nathan Aldyne
Vermilion
(Avon, 1980)

By the 1980's, the critical and commercial success of Joseph Hansen's Dave Brandstetter detective novels encouraged publishers to accept more gay mystery stories, including a popular series by "Nathan Aldyne" (the shared pen-name of Michael McDowell and Axel Young). Avon's edition of *Vermilion*, published toward the end of the Gay Liberation period, shows a young man in a bar being approached by a mysterious stranger. The blurb reads: "The murderer had a weakness for boys...and dirty politics." Ballantine's reprint five years later during the AIDS era, employs the same painting, cropped to make the stranger less prominent and remove the young man's

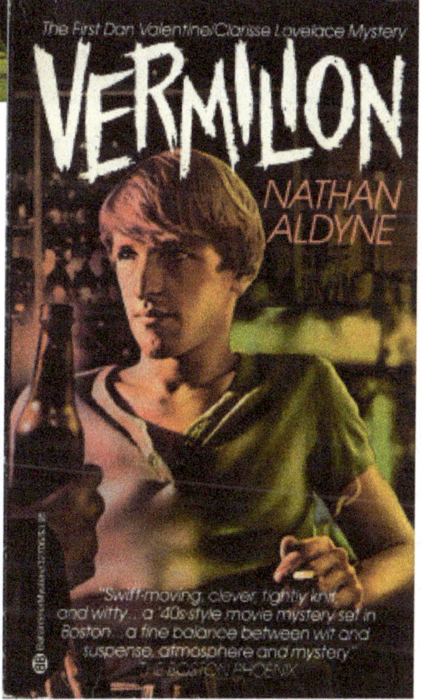

Nathan Aldyne
Vermilion
(Ballantine, 1985)

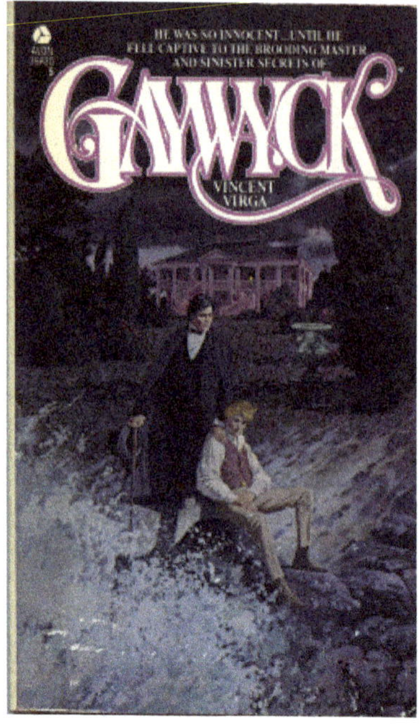

Vincent Virga
Gaywick
(Avon, 1980)

crotch. The new blurb omits the boys - and the politics.

Not only gay detective stories, but gay science fiction, gay fantasy, and even one or two gay westerns made it to the paperback racks. Vincent Virga's gay gothic romance *Gaywick* adapted standard story features of a heretofore heterosexual genre: a beautiful blond teenager travels to a gloomy estate to catalogue the library - and meets a dark, broodingly handsome Irishman "haunted by the dark sexual secrets of his past." Avon's cover duplicates the standard ladies' gothic illustration of the period, with the young woman replaced by a pretty blond male. Even that staple of gothic romance cover art - the single light shining in the window of a dark mansion - has been retained.

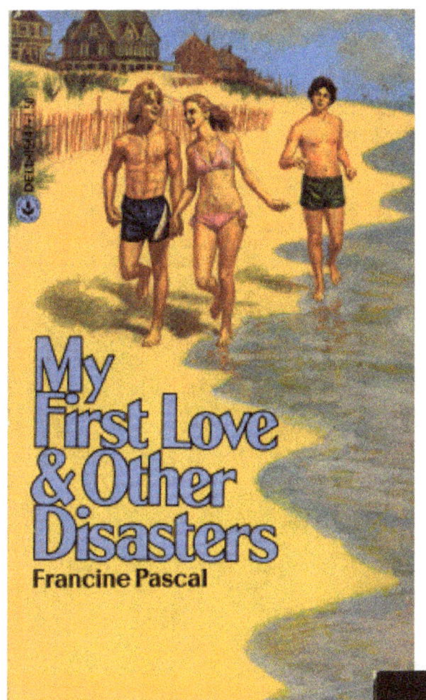

Francine Pascal
My First Love & Other Disasters
(Dell Laurel-Leaf, 1980)

Novels for young adults, particularly young males, often shared cover motifs common to gay novels. Richard Allen's popular series of skinhead novels were much reprinted in the Seventies and Eighties, sometimes with covers showing skinheads with crotches prominently displayed. Francine Pascal's *My First Love & Other Disasters*, intended for teenage girls, shows the two-guys-and-a-girl triangle frequently used for gay novels. It seems clear the second boy will come between the couple - but not at all clear which one he's after. The adventure novels of S.E. Hinton often feature strongly homosocial stories. This film tie-in of *Rumble Fish* shows a popular young actor, a distant silhouette of a boy (with the graffiti slogan "Motorcycle Boy Reigns") and between them a

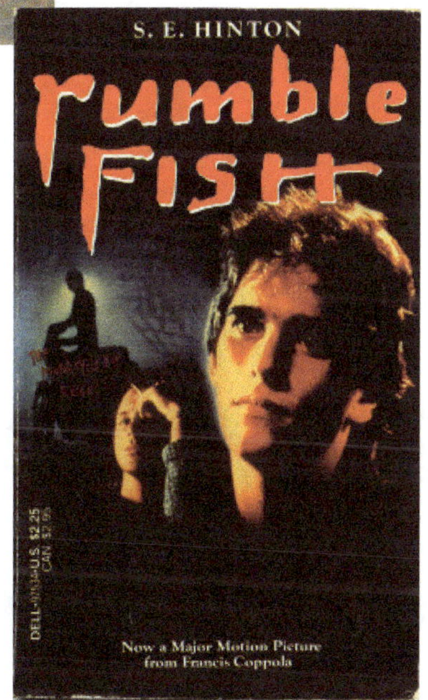

S.E. Hinton
Rumble Fish
(Dell, 1983)

third, sexually ambiguous figure, in an androgynous version of the traditional Triangle. A British TV tie-in edition of Elfreida Read's *Brothers by Choice* shows two young men - one looking at the other who is Looking Away.

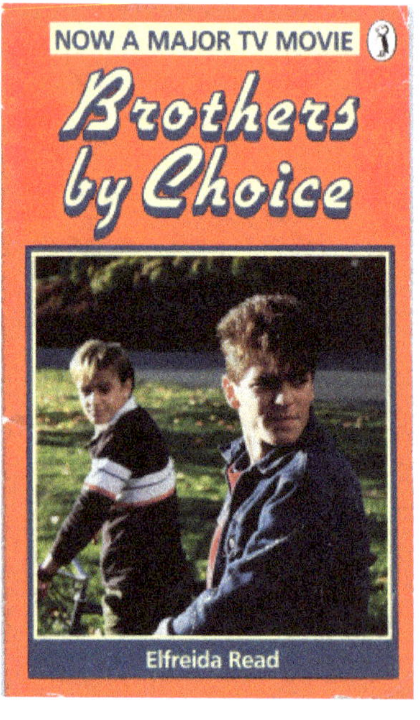

Elfreida Read
Brothers by Choice
(Puffin, 1986)

Ruth Turk's *More Than Friends* and Wallace Hamilton's *Kevin* each dealt with a love affair between a teenaged boy and an older man. Such stories had appeared as far back as the Fifties with Gerald Tesch's *Never the Same Again,* reprinted, abridged, by Pyramid in 1959. In the Eighties, serious novels on the theme could still be respectably published

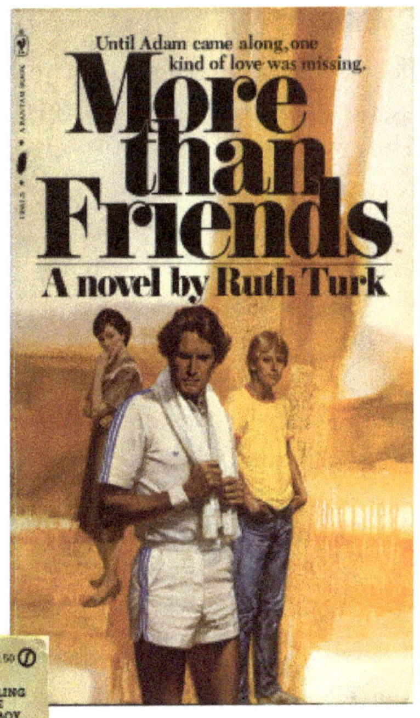

Ruth Turk
More Than Friends
(Bantam, 1980)

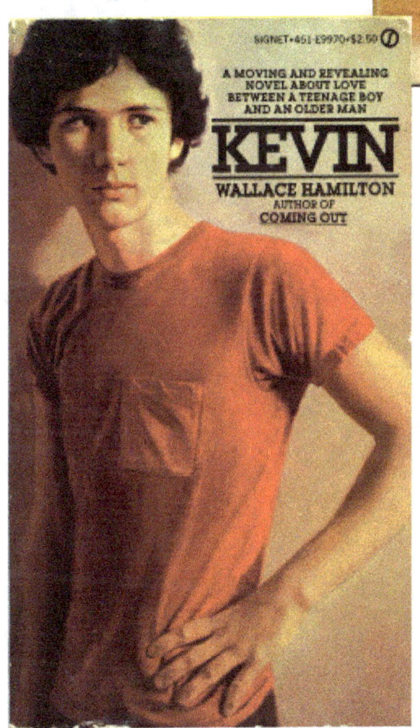

Wallace Hamilton
Kevin
(Signet, 1981)

- and appropriately illustrated. *More Than Friends* relies on the time-honoured Looking Away, Concerned Woman and Triangle motifs, looking old-fashioned by 1980. A note on the verso of *Kevin* hints at nervousness: "Cover painting posed by professional model."

Bruce Ritter's *Sometimes God Has a Kid's Face* is a selection of letters by a

priest to his parishioners about his love for the damaged beauty of the teenage boys he shelters and helps, published by Covenant House, the youth hostel Father Ritter founded. The cover depicts a solitary winsome youth, looking not at the reader but off to the side, perhaps to someone else. Only a few years after *Sometimes God...* was published, the paranoiac sexual politics of the Nineties gave rise to a pedophilia panic that, like a succession of earlier American panics, led to restrictions on the press. In the newly censorious climate, little distinction is made between the affairs of sexually mature teenagers and the molestation of small children. When Father Ritter was found to have had sexual relationships with a number of young men, he was transferred from Covenant House to a Catholic safe house in the country. All copies of his book were removed from the institution he founded, and apparently shipped to thrift stores across the continent.

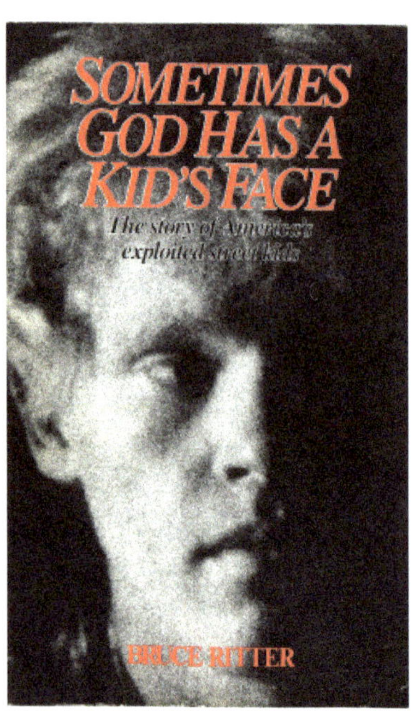

Bruce Ritter
Sometimes God Has a Kid's Face
(Covenant House, 1988)

The Nineties

By the 1990's gay novels were considered acceptable fare by many mainstream publishing houses and their original hardcover, dust-jacketed editions were often reprinted in 8 ½" x 5¼" trade paperback format. Consequently, fewer books of gay fiction showed up as traditional, pocket book format trade paperbacks. Those that did were often erotic stories published by porno houses (most prominently Badboy) or paperback originals of more literary fare. Poet Walter J. Holland's *The March*, a look back at the end of the Gay Lib era and the changes wrought by AIDS, was published as a paperback original by Hard Candy Books - like Badboy, an imprint of Masquerade Books.

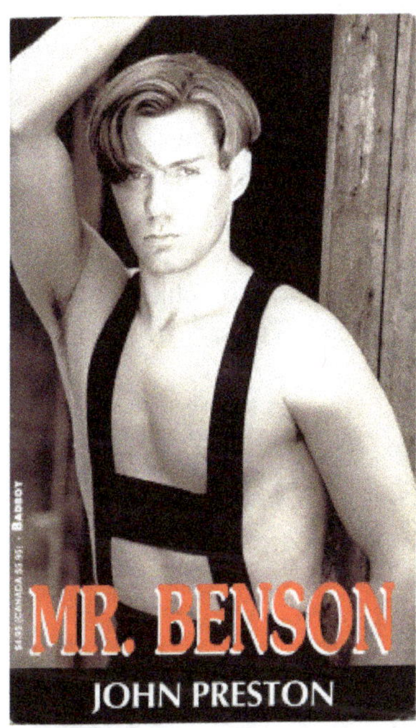

John Preston
Mr. Benson
(Badboy Books, 1992)

A 1992 reprint of John Preston's popular S/M novel *Mr. Benson* (first published in 1980 as a magazine serial over the pen-name Jack Prescott) came adorned with a randomly selected model photo of a shirtless young man wearing a body harness in the shape of the letter H. The abominable Mr. Benson became, fleetingly, a gay icon in the brief "ready for the Eighties" period prior to the onset of AIDS. Benson, a sadistic version of the well-endowed, rich white men in Gordon Merrick's romances, caught the imagination of the gay male public as no Merrick character ever had. T-shirts proclaiming "Looking For Mr. Benson" were worn on Christopher Street and the Castro. Also T-shirts promising: “Mr. Benson.” But that was in the era of “So Many Men, So Little Time” and in the new age of AIDS, the reprinted Mr. Benson was acknowledged as fantasy.

Lars Eighner’s collection of stories *Bayou Boy* showed a solitary young man on a motorbike, a *GQ* model type quite unlike the gritty characters in the stories.

Lars Eighner
Bayou Boy
(Badboy Books, 1993)

The title of Scott O’Hara’s short fiction, *Do It Yourself Piston Polishing (for Non-Mechanics)*, blurbed as “a hands-on guide to the maintenance of the male libido,” gave its own nod to the erotic sway of the machine. O’Hara doubled as his own cover model for the Badboy edition, engaging the reader with a wicked grin,

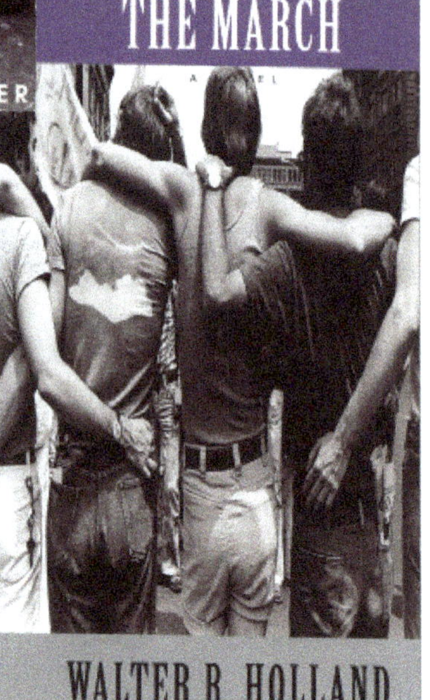

Walter R. Holland
The March
(Hard Candy Books, 1996)

his shirtless body revealing the quintessential Bad Boy emblem of the day - a provocative HIV+ tattoo.

Gay life in the Eighties and early Nineties was dominated by the AIDS crisis and its institutions. AIDS brought more people out of the closet than Gay Lib.

By the end of the Nineties, gay lit had entered the mainstream and gay relationships were accepted - with the proviso that everyone involved be above legal age. A 1994 reprint of Samuel R. Delany's Sixties erotic novel *Equinox* even added a hundred years to "the age of any character in the original version clearly presented as a minor associated with licentiousness"! At the same time, the frequent use of off-the-top-of-the-pile model photos as

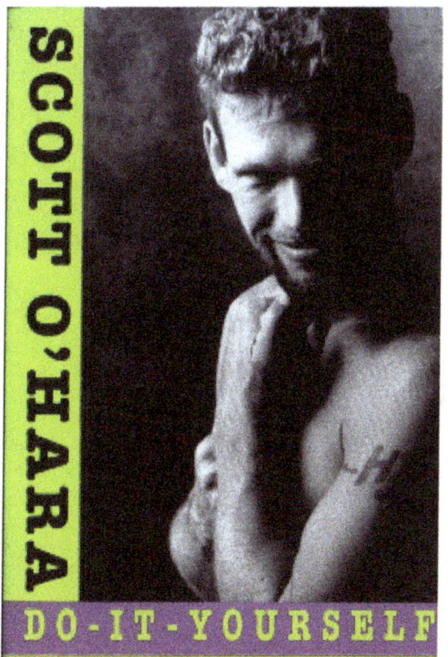

Scott O'Hara
Do-It-Yourself Piston Polishing (for Non-Mechanics)
(Badboy Books, 1998)

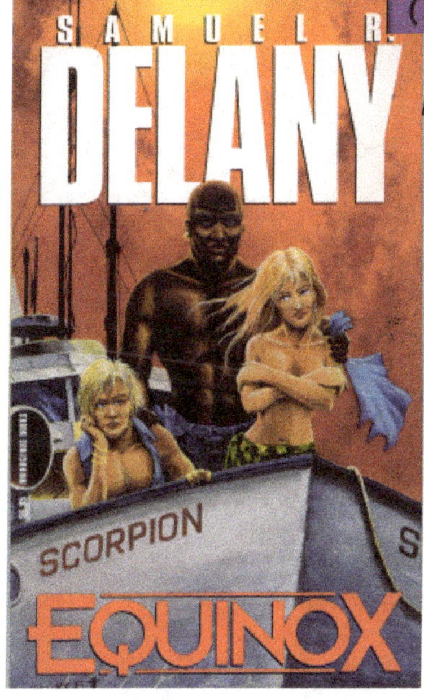

Samuel R. Delany
Equinox
(Rhinoceros, 1994)

cover illustrations suggests publishers had come to regard homosex as simply another standard product to be packaged and promoted by standardized images of young - but not too young - men. Intriguing covers were now more often to be found on larger, more expensive trade publications generating their own economics, their own aesthetic, and their own iconography.

NOTES ON COLLECTING AND COVER ART

It took many years to amass the collection of 1,200 mass-market gay-themed paperbacks that forms the basis of the present study. I acquired them - sometimes for pennies, rarely for more than a few dollars each - from thrift shops, sidewalk vendors, and booksellers' bargain bins. A few were donated by friends. It was an enjoyable quest that in time also proved lucrative once the perceived value of such throwaway treasures began to be more widely appreciated. Most were eventually sold to the Thomas Fisher Rare Book Library at the University of Toronto where they are now available for scholarly study.

The collection includes works by authors as diverse as J.R. Ackerley, James Baldwin, Carl Corley, Samuel R. Delany, Casimir Dukahz, Philip Jose Farmer, Jean Genet, Andre Gide, Paul Goodman, Christopher Isherwood, Thomas Mann, Robin Maugham, Claude McKay, Yukio Mishima, Mary Renault, John Rechy, Theodore Sturgeon, Larry Townsend, Gore Vidal and Oscar Wilde.

Assiduous bargain browsing eventually turned up all four volumes of Richard Armory's Loon Song tetralogy, plus the "Ricardo Amory" parody; all three volumes of David Meltzer's Agency trilogy; all nine gay romances by Gordon Merrick; all five "Billy Farout" novels by poet William Barber; all four school novels by C.J. Bradbury Robinson; both of Kenneth Marlowe's drag queen memoirs; fifteen Joseph Hansen mysteries plus several of his pseudonymous titles; eight of Samuel Steward's "Phil Andros" books; five Marco Vassi novels; and many other intriguing items.

Some of these paperback editions contain material that would be otherwise unavailable, such as blurbs by identified writers or special introductions (e.g. Edmund White's introduction to a new paperback edition of his gay travelogue *States of Desire*, published shortly after the onset of the AIDS crisis). Occasionally, paperback editions embody changes to a book's text - successive paperback editions of Gore Vidal's *The City and the Pillar* saw a number of important textual reworkings, and Angelo d'Arcangelo's *The Homosexual Handbook* was altered to remove the names of J. Edgar Hoover and William F. Buckley, Jr., because of threatened legal actions that followed the first printing.

This study has concentrated on cover art produced by a wide variety of artists and illustrators - some of them very well known - such as James Avati, Don Bachardy, James E. Bama, George Barr, Aubrey Beardsley, Virgil Burnett, Richard Cole, Mario de Graaf, Gerritjan Deunk, Jennifer Eachus, Mort Engel, Max Ernst, Gilbert Fullington, Fisk, Victor Gadino, Edward Gorey, Helmer, David Hockney, Augustus John, Raymond Johnson, Robert Jonas, Cecil Keeling, Liz Moyes, Mel Odom, Barye Phillips, Rex, Ronald Searle, E.H. Shepard, George Stavrinos, Toby, Tom of Finland, Topazio and Vellejo.

One of the most striking things about these (mostly commissioned) covers, it seems to me, is the prevalence of certain motifs, among them the solitary man, suggesting isolation; the triangle of two men and a woman (the equivalent of the two-women-and-a-man triangle on the covers of many lesbian pulps); the concerned or consoling woman; and the looming or lurking man, watching or emerging from a doorway or around a corner. By far the most repeated are the variants of the looking-away motif, the simplest of which shows two men, one of them looking at the other, who is looking away. Homoeroticism here is not reciprocated; when combined with the looming or lurking male figure, it may even be seen as threatening or predatory. One frequent variant is the both-looking-away motif in which two men - with or without a woman - are depicted looking away from each other, suggesting a nonrecognition or denial of attraction. This has proved particularly durable; as late as 2005 it was used for the iconic film poster - and subsequent paperback cover - for Annie Proulx's tragic Western romance, *Brokeback Mountain*.

These recurring motifs are psychologically suggestive - if not always of the actual text of the books then at least of the beliefs and ideas of the artists and publishers who produced them. Below is a listing of possible interpretations for some of the more frequent motifs. For the sake of concision, I have borrowed the term "Homeros" - "a god of homosexuality, Homeros...from the Greek homo = the same + Eros, the love god" from Parker Tyler's *Screening the Sexes: Homosexuality in the Movies*, one of the earliest important studies of homoeroticism in popular culture.

Solitary man - Homeros isolated

Solitary man facing the reader - Homeros acknowledged by reader

One man looking at another who is looking away - Homeros unreciprocated

One man turning to meet another's gaze (cruising) - Homeros acknowledged

Man and woman - Homeros invisible

Two men and a woman - Homeros questioned

Two men looking away from one another - Homeros unacknowledged

Two men facing each other - Homeros mutually acknowledged

Two men facing each other and reaching out - Homeros mutually reciprocated

Two men holding hands - Homeros publicly reciprocated

Two men embracing - Potent Homeros

Two men kissing - Passionate Homeros

Lurking man - Homeros as covert menace

Looming man - Homeros as overt menace

Concerned woman (usually looking down) - Maternal involvement

Disconsolate man - Impotence

Bare-chested man - Courage

Black leather jacket - Rebellion

Indian and white man together - Reconciliation

Peephole - Secret observation

Shadow - Unacknowledged self

Afterword
by David Mason

Anybody over a certain age knows that we rarely get second chances in life; but I'm getting one here.

I was one of the principals of the publishing company which published this book in Canada.

The usual publishing imperatives, time and money, caused us to publish too quickly, before I realized I should have done an introduction to Ian Young's book, because the story behind this book's inception is a story I like a lot.

Ian Young started coming into my bookstore over forty years ago. We gradually went from being bookish friends to friends and we have had probably thousands of conversations over all those years.

One day I found myself talking to Ian about my new passion for collecting vintage paperbacks, especially the Signets of which I read so many as a teenager in the 50s.

I had dropped out of school very early and after work I spent most evenings in the poolroom. On my way home from there I would stop in the corner cigar store where I would buy two or three paperbacks for reading that night. My education, still ongoing, began there, with those books.

Being sixteen or so I was, of course, obsessed by sex so I would naturally seek out the paperbacks whose covers promised sex. Sex sold, then and now, and in their attempts to sell their books paperback publishers often stretched their mandate, both in cover art and blurbs, So that unsuspecting, ignorant young men like me often found themselves actually reading good literature masking itself as soft-core porn to further sales.

My most memorable error was when I bought a lurid-covered book which seemed to promise Roman orgies only to discover Robert Graves' *I, Claudius*. This book literally changed my life, introducing me to the world of ancient Rome and after that the Greeks and then all history.

I never looked back.

When I recounted that anecdote to Ian he laughed and said that he had done the same but that he had had to learn to recognize the code words and the visual signs that the book would have gay appeal.

"The code words? I don't understand," I said.

Ian gave me a lesson. It was still a crime in many places to be gay and that was evident in publishing. Publishers were still testing the market then, wondering how to deal with the increasing reluctance of serious gay writers to mask their character's true orientation. Many people were still in the closet in those days and in fact, one of the saddest things Ian ever told me was that his dream had been to be a teacher, but being openly gay and one of the founders of the first organized gay movement at the University of Toronto, pretty much put an end to that dream for him.

Writers like Gore Vidal and James Baldwin were not prepared to continue the sham of the closet; publishers, respecting the seriousness of their intent, but still frightened by possible crippling legal hassles, used subterfuge.

The book Ian used for my lesson showed a man and woman, the woman unbuttoning her blouse to disrobe.

"No," said Ian, "look closely. She is not undressing; she is dressing. And look at him, he is confused. It hasn't worked, his attempt to fit into straight society has failed and the other man standing in the background signifies what the man must come to terms with. These are the symbols used to inform gays that this is the kind of literature they sought."

I was fascinated, I'd been completely oblivious to those subtle hints. We used that book as the cover of both Ian's book and as the cover illustration on our first catalogue.

"I wrote an essay on the subject," Ian told me. "Would you like to see it?" he said.

I certainly would. And after I read it, I told him I would like to publish his essay, with illustrations. This book is the result.

And to put the icing on the cake, afterwards I sold Ian's large collection of gay paperbacks, on which this book is based, to the University of Toronto, where it now resides, one of the cornerstones of the University's important Sexual Diversities program.

We did very well in Canada with this book and I hope it does as well in the United States.

Along with Ian's earlier bibliographic study *The Male Homosexual in Literature* this book contributes more to the record of the struggle for gay liberation and also to the evolution of popular culture through the making of books.

So while Ian never got to be a teacher he's still teaching.

Bibliography

Adams, Mary Louise. The Trouble with Normal: Postwar Youth and the Making of Homosexuality. Toronto, University of Toronto Press, 1977.

Austen, Roger. Playing the Game: The Homosexual Novel in America. Indianapolis, Bobbs-Merrill, 1977.

Bergman, David. "The Cultural Work of Sixties Gay Pulp Fiction" (in) Patricia Juliana Smith (ed.) The Queer Sixties. NY, Routledge, 1999.

Bonn, Thomas. Under Cover: An Illustrated History of American Mass Market Paperbacks. Harmondsworth, Middlesex, Penguin, 1982.

Bronski, Michael. "Classics from the Closet" (in) *Guide* (February, 1991).

Bronski, Michael. "Fictions About Pulp" (in) *The Gay & Lesbian Review Worldwide* (Vol. VIII, No. 6, November-December, 2001.

Bronski, Michael. Pulp Friction: Uncovering the Golden Age of Gay Male Pulps. NY, St. Martin's Press, 2003.

Cant, Bob and Susan Hemmings (eds.) Radical Records: Thirty Years of Lesbian and Gay History. London, Routledge, 1988.

Clendinen, Dudley and Adam Nagourney. Out for Good: The Struggle to Build a Gay Rights Movement in America. NY, Simon & Schuster, 1999.

Freeman, Gillian. The Undergrowth of Literature. London, Thomas Nelson & Sons, 1967.

Garber, Eric and Lyn Paleo. Uranian Worlds: A Reader's Guide to Alternative Sexuality in Science Fiction and Fantasy. Second edition. Old Tappan, NJ, Macmillan, 1990.

Grier, Barbara (also known as Gene Damon). Lesbiana: Book Reviews from *The Ladder*, 1966 - 1972. Reno, NV, Naiad Press, 1976.

Grier, Barbara. The Lesbian in Literature. Third edition. Tallahassee, FL, Naiad Press, 1981.

Gunn, Drewey Wayne (ed.) The Golden Age of Gay Fiction. Albion, NY, MLR Press, 2009.

Harris, Daniel. "The Evolution of Gay Pornography: Literature" (in) The Rise and Fall of Gay Culture. NY, Hyperion, 1997.

Heller, Steven and Seymour Chwast. Jackets Required: An Illustrated History of American Book Jacket Design, 1920 - 1950. SF, Chronicle Books, 1995.

Keller, Yvonne. "Pulp Politics: Strategies of Vision in Pro-Lesbian Pulp Novels, 1955 - 1965" (in) Patricia Juliana Smith (ed.) The Queer Sixties. NY, Routledge, 1999. .

Koski, Fran and Maida Tilchen. Some Pulp Sappho (in) Karla Jay and Allen Young (eds.) Lavender Culture. NY, New York University Press, 1994.

Miles, Barry. Ginsberg: A Biography. NY, Simon & Schuster, 1989.

Miller, Neil. Out of the Past: Gay and Lesbian History from 1869 to the Present. NY, Vintage, 1995.

Norman, Tom. American Gay Erotic Paperbacks: A Bibliography. Burbank California, Tom Norman, 1994.

Perkins, Michael. The Secret Record: Modern Erotic Literature. NY, William Morrow, 1976.

Schreuders, Piet. The Book of Paperbacks: A Visual History of the Paperback. London, Virgin Books, 1981.

Steward, Samuel M. "The Birth of Phil Andros" (in) Chapters from an Autobiography. SF, Grey Fox Press, 1980

Streitmatter, Rodger. Unspeakable: The Rise of the Gay and Lesbian Press in America. Boston, Faber & Faber, 1995.

Stryker, Susan. Gay Pulp Address Book. SF, Chronicle Books, 2000.

Stryker, Susan. Queer Pulp: Perverted Passions from the Golden Age of the Paperback. SF, Chronicle Books, 2001.

Whitmore, George. "Phil Andros" (in) Ian Young (ed.) Overlooked & Underrated: Essays on Some 20th Century Writers (Little Caesar 12). LA, Little Caesar, 1981.

Woods, Gregory. A History of Gay Literature: The Male Tradition. New Haven, CT, Yale University Press, 1998.

Young, Ian. "How Gay Paperbacks Changed America" (in) *The Gay & Lesbian Review Worldwide* (Vol. VIII, No. 6, November-December, 2001).

Young, Ian. "Lusty! Bawdy! Swaggering! A History of Gay Paperbacks" (in) *Stallion* (October, 1990).

Young, Ian. The Male Homosexual in Literature: A Bibliography. Second edition. Metuchen, NJ, Scarecrow Press, 1982.

Young, Ian. "Sex Gurus of the Seventies: The Legacies of Marco Vassi, Christopher Larkin and Fred Halsted" (in) *Honcho* (November, 1992).

Young, Ian. "Those Notorious Queer Books!" (in) *Torso* (January, 2000).

Zimet, Jaye. Strange Sisters: The Art of Lesbian Pulp Fiction, 1949 - 1969. NY, Viking Studio, 1999.

About the Author

Ian Young is a poet, editor and independent scholar living in Toronto. His books include *The Stonewall Experiment: A Gay Psychohistory, Sex Magick, The Male Homosexual in Literature: A Bibliography* and *The AIDS Cult*. His essays and short stories have appeared in numerous international anthologies including *The Mammoth Book of Gay Short Stories, Serendipity, A Casualty of War, What Love Is, Boys of the Night* and *The Golden Age of Gay Fiction.*

Rainbow Romance Writers

Raising the Bar for LGBT Romance

RRW offers support and advocacy to career-focused authors, expanding the horizons of romance. Changing minds, one heart at a time. www.rainbowromancewriters.com

The Trevor Project

The Trevor Project operates the only nationwide, around-the-clock crisis and suicide prevention helpline for lesbian, gay, bisexual, transgender and questioning youth. Every day, The Trevor Project saves lives though its frce and confidential helpline, its website and its educational services. If you or a friend are feeling lost, alone, confused or in crisis, please call The Trevor Helpline. You'll be able to speak confidentially with a trained counselor 24/7.

The Trevor Helpline: 866-488-7386

On the Web: http://www.thetrevorproject.org/

The Gay Men's Domestic Violence Project

Founded in 1994, The Gay Men's Domestic Violence Project is a grassroots, non-profit organization founded by a gay male survivor of domestic violence and developed through the strength, contributions and participation of the community. The Gay Men's Domestic Violence Project supports victims and survivors through education, advocacy and direct services. Understanding that the serious public health issue of domestic violence is not gender specific, we serve men in relationships with men, regardless of how they identify, and stand ready to assist them in navigating through abusive relationships.

GMDVP Helpline: 800.832.1901

On the Web: http://gmdvp.org/

The Gay & Lesbian Alliance Against Defamation/ GLAAD en Español

The Gay & Lesbian Alliance Against Defamation (GLAAD) is dedicated to promoting and ensuring fair, accurate and inclusive representation of people and events in the media as a means of eliminating homophobia and discrimination based on gender identity and sexual orientation.

On the Web: http://www.glaad.org/

GLAAD en español: http://www.glaad.org/espanol/bienvenido.php

Servicemembers Legal Defense Network

Servicemembers Legal Defense Network is a nonpartisan, nonprofit, legal services, watchdog and policy organization dedicated to ending discrimination against and harassment of military personnel affected by "Don't Ask, Don't Tell" (DADT). The SLDN provides free, confidential legal services to all those impacted by DADT and related discrimination. Since 1993, its inhouse legal team has responded to more than 9,000 requests for assistance. In Congress, it leads the fight to repeal DADT and replace it with a law that ensures equal treatment for every servicemember, regardless of sexual orientation. In the courts, it works to challenge the constitutionality of DADT.

SLDN — Call: 800-538-7418
PO Box 65301 — or (202) 328-FAIR
Washington DC 20035-5301 — e-mail: sldn@sldn.org

On the Web: http://sldn.org/

www.ingramcontent.com/pod-product-compliance
Lightning Source LLC
LaVergne TN
LVHW050539100826
845148LV00002B/615

* 9 7 8 1 6 0 8 2 0 5 6 0 8 *